ENDORSEMENTS FOR

ONLY LOVE

"Niq Ruud's personal stories and reflections provide a path that leads us to a unique understanding of love, care and kindness. *Only Love* stirred my heart, soul and mind as it shows us how God is love whose love for us is unending."

GRACE JI-SUN KIM, PHD
EARLHAM SCHOOL OF RELIGION

"What if we shed the religious distractions to devote ourselves first and foremost to love? And what if we did this as a spiritual adventure, a live experiment, as an exercise in head and heart? I suspect we'd arrive at something like what Niq Ruud offers in this book. I found the adventure in love Ruud describes inviting and his writing winsome. If love matters to you, you'll like this book!"

THOMAS JAY OORD, PHD
AUTHOR OF *GOD CAN'T*

"Stories shape us, even the ones we inherit and the ones we imagine. And, when we lean into the work of re-storying ourselves, as Niq does in his book, we learn that love abounds and the plumb line was and has always been love. This book will help you re-story yourself and get in touch with the work and pattern of love alone. Love is not an ideology in this book; it is a material and discursive power that shapes all of who we are to become."

ROBYN HENDERSON-ESPINOZA, PHD
VANDERBILT UNIVERSITY DIVINITY SCHOOL

"Ruud's whimsical journey through chunky chocolate deluges, tall mountain peaks, and late-night skinny-dips provides readers with an intimate portrait of what love looks like in a messy world, and what our role looks like in helping to clean it up."

CLAY SCROGGINS
AUTHOR OF *HOW TO LEAD WHEN YOU'RE NOT IN CHARGE*

"This book challenges a centuries-old status-quo understanding of the divine. Ruud presents God as nothing more than love, nothing less than love, because he sees God as only love."

SETH PIERCE, PHD
UNION COLLEGE

"The book brilliantly displays the author's life journey in an exciting and easy-reading manner. But his story has a clear message: the love of Jesus for anyone, which flows through a loving relationship. And this love looks for the marginalized and neglected, bringing hope, light, and new meaning. The climax of this message is that no other love but Jesus' restores and transforms life. The book embodies this beautiful love, and it will touch and impact countless people."

JULIE MA, PHD
ORAL ROBERTS UNIVERSITY

"*Only Love* manages to do what so many books wish they could do but often don't. It not only entertains, but edifies. It embodies love and pushes it out beyond its pages. Niq's gripping stories and skillful theological reflections help to create a work, born of love, that not only remains memorable, but inspiring. Do yourself a favor and read this book!"

MATTHEW J. KORPMAN
AUTHOR OF *SAYING NO TO GOD*

"Ruud expresses a willingness to meet readers right where they are in order to convince them of this one thing, God loves them that way. A crafted storyteller, he takes each of us figuratively by the hand and walks us to the gospel of Jesus Christ."

TRACI RHOADES
AUTHOR OF *NOT ALL WHO WANDER (SPIRITUALLY) ARE LOST*

"Niq's words will disrupt your thought patterns in the wittiest and most nurturing of ways. So many want to change the world for good, yet, this quest can leave us overwhelmed by viral posts, protests, and Amazon book addictions. As an alternative, Niq invites us to a much simpler, yet sacred, often overlooked path; a path rarely even taken by the church itself. Prepare yourself and/or your small group for this book to not only improve your confidence in who God made you to be but to also improve your hearing toward who God is calling you and the world to become."

MEGGIE LEE CALVIN
AUTHOR OF *I AM MY OWN SANCTUARY*

"Each chapter in Niq Ruud's *Only Love* begins with a personal story (describing the author's childhood, outdoor adventures, experience of college life and early adulthood—and even trips to Taco Bell) that help to illustrate his theology. In short, Ruud believes that simple, transformative concept that God is love. Readers in need of help untangling their faith and their image of God from harmful or toxic theology and who long to know One who 'only loves' will find comfort and relief in this book."

JENNIFER GRANT
AUTHOR OF *LOVE YOU MORE*

ONLY

HOW EVERYTHING
WAS, IS, AND
WILL BE

LOVE

NIQ RUUD

Copyright © 2021 by Niq Ruud.

Cover design and layout by Rafael Polendo (polendo.net)
Cover illustration by morokey (storyblocks.com)

First Edition

Scripture quotations from the Old Testament are taken from the New Revised Standard Version Bible, copyright © 1989 National Council of the Churches of Christ in the United States of America. Used by permission. All rights reserved worldwide.

Scripture quotations from the New Testament are taken from The New Testament: A Translation, copyright © 2017 by David Bentley Hart. Used by permission of Yale University Press. All rights reserved.

ISBN 978-1-938480-98-0

This volume is printed on acid free paper and meets ANSI Z39.48 standards.
Printed in the United States of America

Published by Quoir
Oak Glen, California
www.quoir.com

CONTENTS

For Jo

Who each day expands my understanding of the divine;
I can appropriately say that you are only love to me.

Darkness cannot drive out darkness; only light can do that. Hate cannot drive out hate; only love can do that.[1]

— Martin Luther King Jr

---

1   Martin Luther King Jr, *Strength to Love*, 47.

FOREWORD

The spiritual journey is anything but straight and narrow, despite what the fire-and-brimstone preachers on television would have us to believe.

The spiritual journey is a winding road that for many of us begins with a desperate search for stability and hope, then gradually evolves into certainty, and eventually, as our certainty dissolves, we find ourselves left with only two options: wonder or nihilism.

When I began my journey as a teenager, I was deeply lost. Even at a young age, I felt that life was meaningless, that I was unlovable, and that any chance of living a full life was well beyond my reach. But then, I encountered *love.*

At the time, I would have said it was the love of God, expressed through Jesus, and accessed through believing the right things about who Jesus was and what he did on earth. The truth is that the justification and explanation of how I encountered love was irrelevant—the fact is that I, as a young soul starved of any sense of value, encountered a love that began to heal my deepest wounds and spark a sense of possibility for what my life could become.

Later on, as my now certainty-based faith began to be shaken by my experience of reality, it was *love* that kept me stable. I began to realize that regardless of whether what I believed was right or wrong, that love was constant and enduring. Nothing could separate me from it. No matter what doubts I entertained, what questions I asked, and what conclusions I ended up at. Love was my singular unshakable foundation.

And today, as I sit writing these words, more sure than ever that any of the answers I can give about the meaning of life, the existence of God, the hope of the afterlife are all destined to fall short of truth, I can only sit in absolute amazement that it is *love* that has endured every trial, every failure, and the complete reconfiguration of my spiritual path.

Love alone has remained.

The Book of 1 John tells us that God's fundamental nature is love, and that God is the very ground of our existence, the animating force that permeates all things. If this is true, it means that there is nowhere we can go—physically or spiritually—that is not saturated with love.

That same passage which describes God's nature as love also tells us that anyone who truly *knows God* will necessarily reflect that deep knowing through loving others.

It also says that anyone who knows love will have the fears within them cast aside, because love is the guarantee that absolutely everything will somehow ultimately be okay.

Therein lies the power of love. Therein lies the true message at the heart of the Jesus story and nearly every other spiritual tradition.

Love is all that there is. Love is all that will be. Love alone is real.

The book you're holding is a powerful testimony to this fact. Niq Ruud invites us to join him on his own spiritual journey, leading us with wit, sincerity, and a profound vulnerability to help us come to see the pervasive presence of love in our own lives and in our world.

The love Ruud introduces us to is not a sentimentalized version of love, but a love that leads us to transform our lives and our world around us for the good of the oppressed, the marginalized, and the outcast. It's a love that refuses to accept the world as it is because it dares to dream of the world that can be. It's a love that is rooted in the teachings and example of Jesus of Nazareth, a love that is completely within our ability to experience and to embody.

Here, at the beginning of this truly inspiring book, I want to encourage you to prepare to be shaken—in the best way possible. Ruud's journey and perspective will challenge you to your core, invite you to rethink the way you have understood and experienced the call to be loving, and ultimately lead you into a deeper experience of the one thing that is ultimately real ... you guessed it, *love*.

I am so grateful for Niq Ruud's work and witness, and I am so glad you've picked up this book.

Let us begin the journey of *Only Love.*

— **Brandan Robertson**
author of *Nomad: A Spirituality for Traveling Light*

PART ONE

HOW GOD WAS, IS, AND WILL BE

1

BEFORE WE BEGIN

I'm not convinced that the god I grew up worshiping exists.

I've read many brilliant and convincing arguments against the divine, most of which are as sound as can be. In perhaps one of my favorites, the vehemently anti-religious scholar, Richard Dawkins, says this of the supernatural:

> A theist believes in a supernatural intelligence who, in addition to his main work of creating the universe in the first place, is still around to oversee and influence the subsequent fate of his initial creation ... the deity is intimately involved in human affairs. He answers prayers; forgives or punishes sins; intervenes in the world by performing miracles; frets about good and bad deeds, and knows when we do them.[2]

Statements like this, particularly when read in the near sarcastic tone Dawkins intends, test my faith in the god I grew up learning about—perhaps they test yours, too. I remember sitting with my family on a bright green couch gifted to us by my great-grandmother, singing hymns about marching in God's army and flying o'er the enemy. I recall hearing from the pulpit of my fundamentalist Christian church that God was something like a divine Kris Kringle. He was a "he" who knew what I was doing and was keeping track, so I had better be a good person if I wanted to get good things. I remember feeling guilty,

---

2 Richard Dawkins, *The God Delusion*, 39.

dirty, disgusting, and even worthless at times. This god seemed so distant, so selfish, so perfect, so complex. I hated this god. God sucked.

I liked Jesus, though.

Unlike his Old Testament counterpart, Jesus didn't go around seemingly initiating genocides. Instead, he was the subject of one.[3] Jesus was relatable. He had personality—flair. He was complex and supposedly perfect, yes, but also approachable and really quite human. Not as seemingly egotistical, instead, he was humble and really quite kind. And because Jesus seemed to be so cool, I pretty much limited my biblical reading to Matthew, Mark, Luke, and John for a good number of my years as a young, Christian boy. In all honesty, I couldn't have cared less about the rest of the Bible. While I'm now most certainly past the point where a collection of ancient poems, histories, myths, and metaphors serve as the exclusive moral parameter by which I live my life, when they did, I came across this verse in John where Jesus is quoted as saying, "Have faith in me, that I am in the Father and that the Father is in me."[4]

Suddenly, the rest of scripture appeared quite interesting. I grew up hearing the classic trinitarian talking point that God the Father, Jesus, and the Holy Spirit were one-in-the-same. But this verse spelled it out clearly: God, in God's infiniance, chose to relate to humans *through* Jesus. In Jesus, God became visible, knowable, touchable, *real*. And if that supposition were true, Jesus had to be God. And since Jesus came as a human, who got tired, thirsty, hungry, and had to poop just like me, he would be as close as my mind will ever come to comprehending what and who this God character is really like. Jesus, then, could serve as our imaginable example of an unimaginable God.

---

3   Matthew 2:16.

4   John 14:11.

Our best example of what God does and our best example of what God says. Because Jesus was and is God.

When I took those first steps towards such an understanding, I got even more excited about Jesus. Jesus wasn't just cool anymore, Jesus was God![5] As different as Jesus and God might seem, humans hadn't truly *seen* God until Jesus arrived on the scene. I read more and more, realizing this Jesus guy was, really, just like me. He had a huge personality, yet seemed so balanced. He could talk all day with thousands of people, yet needed to escape the crowds when his emotional tank was running low. He could call out injustices of the various social, political, and religious systems around him, and scare hundreds out of the ancient Jews' third temple, yet walked everywhere, hundreds and hundreds of kilometers, day after day, on dusty roads. In sandals no less!

If you ask me, that's a special kind of special.

In my sophomore year of high school, I remember a teacher having my fellow classmates and I take the Meyers-Briggs personality test. When he first presented the idea, it was met with some backlash—I mean it sounded like wretched standardized testing all over again! Yet we, reluctantly, sat down for the hour and answered page after page of questions like: "Do you enjoy vibrant social events with lots of people, or would you rather read a book at home?" or, "If your friend is sad about something, is your first instinct to support them emotionally or to try and solve their problem?" or one of my personal favorites, "Do

---

5 I love how Greg Boyd puts this in his book, *Inspired Imperfection*, 65: "Jesus is God revealing Godself *in person.*"

people really upset you?" Because, well, an answer to that question totally depends on *everything*.

The next day, our teacher had the results assessed and ready for us to view—so we spent the class period talking about what each letter meant. "E" was equated to "extrovert," while "I" represented introverted characteristics, and so on. He had prepared several pages of informative material for each student, which explained our various personalities, and we all took the hour to learn about ourselves based on our results. Those few moments were actually quite eye-opening for me as I've always used different mental categories to help compartmentalize the world around me. So, giving labels to various elements of personality was awesome! (Especially when it came to exploring the personalities of my classmates and teachers.)

At the end of the period, my teacher, a Christian, said something which has stuck with me since: "Jesus had the perfect personality."

The *perfect* personality? That sparked my attention. He went on to say that Jesus had the most balanced personality, encapsulating all personality traits, and understanding ourselves, our own personalities, subsequently aids in our understanding of his. Now, while this Jesus guy, traditionally said to be God in the flesh, was bound by human restrictions like gender, culture, time, and religious creed, what stands out to me as being so perfect about his personality is that it was only love. That's it. Nothing more. Nothing less. Perfectly balanced. *Only love*.

I think a little letter by John spells it out pretty clearly: "God is love, and whoever abides in love abides in God, and God abides in him"[6] I, for lack of a better word, *love* the interchangeability of "God"

---

6   1 John 4:16. While I acknowledge the breadth of debate regarding the authorship of various fragments of the biblical text, I am no historian. So I will, throughout this book, attribute a work's authorship to whom it is traditionally credited.

and "love" as outlined by the biblical author because this God of love seems so different from the god I was raised to worship. That god was something closer to 96.78 percent love. Now don't get me wrong, that's still a lot of love. I mean I'm probably sitting at around 1.82 percent love myself; but I think the philosopher Thomas Talbott perfectly puts words to what I'm driving at here when he says, "Anything less than a perfectly loving God ... would be far worse than no God at all."[7] Meaning that the only God worth even a moment of our time is a God of only love—as in *100 percent*. Not simply a God who loves, but a God who is love itself.

Now, full disclosure here—and you might have already supposed this—I do, on most days, categorize myself as a Christian. (Remember, I like to compartmentalize things.) So, while I certainly don't condone the vast majority of things my faith tradition has done over the past 2000 years, or even the past twenty, I honestly can't help myself from being a Jesus-follower, Christ-follower, Christian, whatever you want to call it. Because, get this, Jesus spells out what it means to be a Christian quite clearly: Christians are those who strive to follow the greatest commandment, so as to carry out the greatest commission.

I get it—that might sound like a lot of boring religious jargon to you, but hear me out on this one. The greatest commandment is to love—to only love. The gospel writer Mark records Jesus saying, "'And you shall love the Lord your God out of your whole heart and out of your whole soul and out of your whole reason and out of your whole strength.' The second is this: 'You shall love your neighbor as yourself.' There is not another commandment greater than these."[8] Love is it. Love is what we're tasked with. *Only love.* But what about

7 Thomas Talbott, *The Inescapable Love of God*, 7.

8 Mark 12:30-31.

the great commission? How are we to go about living in that greatest commandment of only love? Jesus goes on to outline this for us as well: "Go, therefore, instruct all the nations, baptizing them in the name of the Father and the Son and the Holy Spirit, teaching them to observe everything that I have commanded you."[9] He's saying to baptize everyone in the names of God, in the name of love, and then teach them his own command, which, yeah, you already know, was to love! To put it simply: the great commandment in conjunction with the great commission calls us to only love.

To take this a step further, if Jesus-followers are those who strive to follow the greatest commandment so as to carry out the great commission, this would mean that Christians are simply those who love. Meaning you can be a Jesus-follower, a "Christian," without even knowing it. It also means you don't have to go to church three out of every four weekends or count yourself as "religious" to be a Christian either. In fact everyone who has ever loved—which, dare I say, is *everyone*—might just be Christian. If that's not an all-inclusive hope-filled message, I don't know what is. As Augustine once put it: "For what is now called the Christian religion existed even among the ancients and was not lacking from the beginning of the human race."[10] He expresses the thought that people have intrinsically, magically been able to love like Jesus since way before he came and lived a life filled with only love. As in the love that God is participates universally.

Several places in the Christian scriptures attest to this as well: Paul says that God communicates without boundaries and David sings that there is no place where the language of God goes unheard.[11] Reading

---

9   Matthew 28:19-20.

10   Augustine, *The Retractions*, 52.

11   See Romans 1:19-20; Psalm 19:3.

this into our modern context, I think it means you can experience love without ever calling it "God," or without ever labeling it "Jesus." You may very well have known Jesus' love by another name or another face, but that doesn't make the love you've encountered any less divine. You could easily be an agnostic or an atheist and have experienced divine love just as I or any other religious person with the supposed "right" language has.

Because of this, it is my hope that this book provides us with both fresh and succinct nomenclature for how we go about defining what and who God is. As science has progressed through the ages, so too has our understanding of God and the heavens. It was not long ago that our ancestors saw the sky above and assumed they were living in a snowglobe of sorts, with gods looking down from above the dome; the earth was flat and turtles were holding up it's foundations. As our species' understanding of the world around us grew beyond these limitations, so, too, did our understanding of the divine. Yet in the past 100 years, since theoretical physicists have introduced ideas such as string theory and quantum entanglement, our perspective of God has all too often remained stagnant—unmoved as science and culture push onward without it. It is time again to reimagine God.

So, here at the beginning of this journey, just to be forthright, I am speaking through the lens of my faith tradition to convey this reimagined vision of God—and can you blame me? That's all I really know! But I want to be clear: I'm using the language of Christianity in an attempt to transcend Christianity. In my tradition, many of us see Jesus, the guy with the perfect personality, as the uttermost epitome of love. Divine love in human form—the kind of love that never says it owns something, although it owns everything; the kind of love that never says, "This is mine" or "That is mine," but rather, "All that is mine is yours."[12] The really amazing thing is that Christians often see Jesus as someone who gives every person the same infinite and never-ending opportunity to join in his divine dance, even if we don't have the "correct" verbiage for it all.

Because of my desire to cast a more inclusive vision of what God is in this book, you may notice what might sound like a bit of awkward language when it comes to pronoun usage as attributed to God. I've chosen to use God/Godself rather than the traditional he/him/his as I want us to remember who we are talking about when we talk about God: the God which the author of Genesis assumes is beyond constraints like time ("in the beginning"), matter ("God created"), and space ("the heavens and in earth") in which what we call gender exists.[13] Calling God a "he" is more of a commonly-used and quite ancient metaphor than anything else; and to remind us of this, perhaps we ought use genderless pronouns for the divine more often. For as love certainly transcends the limits of gender, so, too, does God.

Seeing God in this transcendent way is important because it opens up a valuable framework which suggests that if God moves in the world now, our stories matter. As in your and my experiences are just as important as the experiences of those recorded in scripture—how love interacts and intersects with you and your life is just as valuable as how love interacted and intersected with ancient authors of millennia ago. So in this book, I'm going to tell stories—lots of stories! The narratives I'll share have helped frame who and what God is for me, and I'm hoping they may do the same for you. Sometimes we give Christianity's collection of ancient texts far more weight than we

---

12 Paraphrased from the Gospel of Philip.

13 See Genesis 1:1.

really ought. Jesus even goes so far as to bash those who think they have found God in the academic exercise of studying scripture.[14] I think he saw the holy collection as a launching pad through which we can ground our own holy experience—not something which we worship *as* god. Frankly, I'd prefer we focus our attention on God as something which persuades us to be love now, because love was, is, and will always be the thing which binds all things.

Leveling with you for a moment, however, I have close to zero qualifications when it comes to writing a book about the personality of God as being only love. Because, well, if I'm going to be honest, I'm pretty bad at loving most of the time. Just ask my partner, or my dad, or my sister. They know my unloving nature better than just about anyone. And as much as I might try, I've come to a place where I'm okay knowing I'll never fully have the capacity to be only love as Jesus is portrayed as having been. I guess that would be crazy anyway and pretty arrogant if I thought I could. But when I look at the overarching metanarrative of the Bible, I really do see God as being other-centered, self-sacrificial, only love. The kind of love worthy of my attention and adoration—*a God who is love in all.*

But just because I'm not wholly love, doesn't mean love isn't at work in my life. In fact, I see it all around me, all of the time. Let me just say that I like to think I can recognize some good lovin' when I see it. But it's not always blatantly obvious; sometimes I've really got to seek it out. Yet, even in the times when I have had to look really hard, and even in the times when I haven't noticed it at first, that doesn't mean love wasn't there, under the surface, waiting to be revealed all along. For love is as simple as a kiss, and as complex as a romance. As pure as water yet as unpredictable as the ocean. Love

---

14 John 5:39.

can be furious and funny but also humble and silent. I have glimpsed it, and when I do, I always want more because it's just that beautiful.

- ♡ -

Like I said earlier, I'm not convinced the god I grew up worshiping even exists. In fact, I hope that god doesn't.

But I know love exists.

So let's talk about love—*only love.*

2

A NOSE THAT WORKS

The name's Niq, Niq Ruud, and I can smell.

I know people usually like to start off book chapters with a brilliant epigraph from somebody famous or something. Good for them, maybe that's why they make the *New York Times* bestseller list. But I figure that I might as well start off with a confession instead. Because, as they say, "confession is good for the soul."

I can smell.

Granted, this may not be the most exciting way to start, but I just wanted to get that off my chest early on. Because beginning the summer of my thirteenth birthday, I decided to see if I could lie about something long enough to make it actually happen. I wanted to see if I could fib something into reality. And so I chose to lie about my sense of smell. I wanted to see if lying about not being able to smell would eventually translate into losing my sense of smell altogether.

I know, it's stupid. But let me explain.

To my thirteen-year-old brain, smell was one of those useless senses. Because, for the most part, you can get along just fine in modern society without it. Let's say I had decided to fake blindness—well I would have had to procure a walking cane and learn to read in braille—that would be pretty hard. Or say I had chosen sound—I would have had to teach myself not to jump when someone says, "Boo!" and probably would have needed to learn sign language as well—again, pretty difficult to pull off. So, knowing that both of those options would have been real logistical nightmares, I chose smell. Simple. Easy. And most importantly, easy.

For eight years my little experiment went off without disruption.

Early on, Mom and Dad took me to a special smell doctor who had me sniff funny potions and the like. But I had to keep my secret safe, so I just faked it no matter how bad or weird the scents. (Actually, right here from the get-go, I should mention how deeply sorry I am for those med bills, Mom and Dad. Like really, *really* sorry. I'm so sorry that I'm mentioning my remorse here in print. There are tears on my keyboard!) Well, long story short, I somehow justified this parental pick-pocketing by saying that it was "in the name of science." No matter my rationale, there I was, a thirteen-year-old kid sitting in the nose doctor's office. Whenever he had me sniff something smelly, I simply claimed I couldn't. It was as easy as eating apple pie while watching a summer's sunset!

Next, I needed a backstory. I used my history with hay fever—which indeed limited my sense of smell seasonally—as a point of origin. It was perfect. Lastly, I had to make the lie a habit. When people said, "Oh doesn't that paper plant just smell terrible?!" or "I do love me some petunias!", I taught myself to reply, "Oh, really? Does that dog poo turn up your nose? That's incredible! Because I can't seem to make it out!" The lie was gaining traction.

Sure, people had their doubts, especially when I would insist, sarcastically of course, that everything anyone put under my nose smelled like "flowers." But for the most part, I got away with it.

I remember one time in high school when my sense of smell betrayed the lie I had been telling. A couple of friends and I were driving back home from grabbing a bite to eat at Taco Bell, you know, the place my partner affectionately calls "Taco Smell." I was riding shotgun in my friend's tricked-out black Mustang. Or was it a Dodge? I can't remember exactly. Dark leather seats, stick shift, a sky window that actually worked, you get the picture. It was a pretty slick ride compared to my Goodwill rollerblades.

Anyway, a few kilometers out, we decided to take a detour on the gravel roads past the local cemetery. A kilometer up the road, my buddy decided it would be a great idea to relinquish his position as driver for that of a spectator in the rear of the car. So the rear passenger, my future college roommate, switched seats with him to become the driver. The now backseat driver relaxed, thinking his sweet ride was in the hands of a professional. Sadly, it wasn't. The wheels spun viciously while the brake pads remained firmly on the rotor. My brain shut off and my mouth turned on as I said, "Oh, that smells terrible!" Because, well, it did.

The secret was out. And I was scrambling for a solution.

What I should have done was spoken in a sarcastic sonnet, quickly playing off my mistake as a joke: "Oh, that smells terrible … like flowers!" But instead, I took the tumultuous way out and insisted that I most certainly had smelt the rubber. Then, only moments later, I suddenly claimed I wasn't able to smell it or anything else anymore! What a brilliant solution! What a master manipulator I had become!

"Losing" my sense of smell wasn't the first time I fabricated a lie in the name of "science." I used to pretend that electrical lines gave me migraines. Yeah, they gave me these five-second headaches as I passed under them in a car. Even before that, around the age of nine or so, I would smash my leg or arm really hard against my bunk bed so that it would swell-up a little bit, and I could claim it was broken. Subsequently, this allowed me to sport a really cool glow-in-the-dark cast which I would keep on for a few weeks until it lost its novelty, "accidentally" got wet, and was buzzed off by my dad's skilled saw.

It's crazy what we humans will do to get attention! And I know I'm not the only one. Look around! Crazy (albeit sometimes pretty cool) haircuts. Ridiculously pricey shoes and clothes. New cars with next year's date. A more important title or job description. That advanced degree. Working out until those biceps are the size of my head! Makeup galore. And lies just like mine—the list goes on.

Another time, while in high school, I guess I figured that sweet sixteen must just be the sweetest of ages. So, I made sure that I was sixteen for three years straight. Freshman year I was "sixteen" years old. As a sophomore again I was sixteen (but for real that time). And by the time my Junior year came around, I was, once again, "sixteen." Nobody caught on or at least cared enough to confront me about it. Not until senior year, when I suddenly jumped two years in age to eighteen, did I get a few confused looks. Much to my internal delight.

All I wanted, since bashing my leg against my bunk bed for the first time, was attention. Sometimes we humans want attention more than we want anything else. I think Brené Brown is spot-on in saying that, because people can't always articulate how they feel, "they show us by acting out, thinking, *This will get their attention.*"[15]

The truly amazing thing about all of those lies I told is how much my parents, classmates, and friends, if they ever caught on, loved me through them all. Not once did anyone tell me I was wrong, even if they were aware of my fabrication; they instead chose to play along with my little games. Questioning my sanity, yes, I have no doubt, but always loving me through it in the most radical of ways.

---

15 Brené Brown, *Daring Greatly*, 52.

Truth be told, I didn't tell anyone about my actually being able to smell until I was twenty-one, eight years after the lie had first been born. And even after that, I kept it a secret from nearly everyone in my life well into my twenties. Whether they were conscious of my fibs or not, my family and friends showed me a glimpse of how much the God I believe in loves each one of us. In a very real way, in their love for me, they were God to me.

You see, the God I'm working to see, the God I'm trying to frame for us in this book, the one who we're told lives inside of each and every human out there; that God doesn't seem to care all that much how many times we lie to God and to ourselves.[16] It seems to me that this God is well aware we're simply trying to make ourselves look better, gain a bit of attention, or feel better about who we are. And the brilliant thing is this God is there to love us through it. No matter who you are. No matter what.[17] Because I think God becomes real when love is conscious amongst us.

Jesus, Christianity's example of divine love in human form, was extremely inclusive. And when I say "extremely," I mean *extremely*. There is this great little story in John's gospel which most anyone who's spent time in Christian circles knows of, but many don't know all that much about. Jesus had been on a walk with his pals, and while they headed to a market to grab some grub, he hung out on the edge of town where he met a woman: "Jesus says to her, 'Give me a drink.' For his disciples had gone away into the city so that they might buy

---

16 Galatians 2:20; Romans 8:10; 2 Corinthians 13:5.

17 Clark Pinnock makes a case for this in his essay, "An Inclusivist View," in *Four Views on Salvation in a Pluralistic World*, 98.

food. So the Samaritan woman says to him, 'How do you, being a Judaean, ask for a drink from me, a Samaritan woman?'"[18]

I think most of the time most of us would breeze right past this bit because, well, I'm not a Jew or a Samaritan, and I kind of doubt you are either, nor are we all that conscientious about being alone, in broad daylight, with someone of a variant gender. But things were a lot different in Palestine a couple thousand years ago. What makes this interaction so interesting is that Jews despised Samaritans, like they wouldn't even talk to them. Seriously! The Samaritans were this group of "impure" Hebrew step-siblings from the north. They hadn't kept God's rules quite as vigorously as their southern neighbors, especially when it came to things like interracial marriage. So, not only was there a severe racial tension but also a certain stigma as Jesus, a man, was talking to a woman—and a Jewish man would never speak to a Samaritan woman.[19] It was seen as being totally wrong in that cultural context. Reading further we learn that he wasn't just talking to any woman, but a woman who, in that wholly patriarchal world, had been carelessly tossed from one man to the next, garnering divorce after divorce.[20] Society would have seen her as worthless. Yet, Jesus spoke to her. In fact, he didn't just speak *to* her, he spoke *with* her. The two of them have a conversation where anyone and everyone could easily see them! How shameful of Jesus, right? How scandalous!

Perhaps the woman was desperate for affirmation. I mean she, without any societal rights, had already been tossed through five marriages, and Jesus, without question, gives her exactly what she is fishing for—what she truly needed so as to be seen. Jews and Samaritans

---

18 John 4:7-9.

19 N.T. Wright & Michael Bird, *The New Testament in Its World*, 667-668.

20 John 4:18.

weren't even supposed to eat with the same utensils, and yet Jesus is totally fine taking a drink from her water jug. He doesn't care for one second that he isn't supposed to be hanging with her due to race, gender, or otherwise, because Jesus was of a radically inclusive breed. And being that Jesus was and is a part of God, we readers are keyed into the truth that this affirming characteristic is a part of the character of love that God is said to be. God is unconditional affirmation. Unconditional love. Unearned love. Unmerited love. Undeserved love. Universal love. *Only love.*

Jesus, the human manifestation of the divine, came with this single goal in mind: to love. And sometimes his affirming love was accomplished in an act as simple as asking for a drink of water. But it's not just Jesus that was and is love, because he encouraged all of us to dig deep inside of ourselves and discover the same kind of love inside of *us*. It's that practice of digging that this book is all about. That we get to join in this beautiful exchange of give and take, a divine dance as it were. Seeking-out love, Jesus' whole mission summed-up in a word. And subsequently, the highest calling of a human like you or me.

And, of course, we'll run into problems, most of which we make for ourselves. It's unavoidable as a human. I mean think about it: we humans even want to make God fit into our own little boxes. We see God as we wish to see God, not as God tells us God is: gracious, merciful, and loving.[21] A crazy example of this is found in the story of the ancient Hebrews just freed from slavery by their invisible God when they try to make the very same God visible![22] They make a golden calf, something they could understand coming from the context of Egypt,

---

21 See Exodus 34:6-7. Many people are challenged by the latter half of verse seven, to which I would recommend a short video by Tim Mackie & Jon Collins, "Character of God: Exodus 34:6-7," *BibleProject*.

22 Exodus 32:2-4.

and call it "YHWH."[23] They call something they made "God." God even told them not to do this at the beginning of the playbook God offered them, because God wanted the Hebrews to know that their God was not limited in the ways humans are, for God's very nature is that of infinite mercy, grace, and love—something which a shiny metallic cow doesn't exactly convey.

Too often I think we get the word "love" all mixed-up with the idea of butterflies and unicorns. And yes, looking at Jesus, he loved by lifting up the oppressed, hanging out with the marginalized just like his friend at the well, chatting with "sinners," and doing all of those great things. But Jesus also loved by working to flip the idea of religion on its head. He quite literally came and turned things upside down and inside out. And when he did that, everything changed. Jesus said that the last are now first and the first are last. The dismissed are chosen and the chosen are dismissed. The sinners are holy and the holy are proved to be sinners. Those who thought they understood love are actually pretty lost, and those who were thought to be lost are actually incredibly loved.

If you ask me, God still loves in that radical, upside down, affirming way. Because the very essence of God is that of love. And a little birdy once told me that God even loves folks who lie about the functionality of their olfactory system. I, for one, think that's pretty amazing.

Only love smells pretty sweet.

---

23 Exodus 32:4.

3

THE TOOTH FAIRY'S TALL TALE

My parents, too, seemed to love in a radical and upside-down way while I was growing up. For instance, forcing me to sport a mohawk, perform an entire concert with my sister at the county fair, or eat broccoli. But other than those upside-down methods of love, the first ten years of my growing up were pretty great.

My dad had steady work, and although he was no longer the mortician he had always dreamed of being, the jobs he did have paid well enough and, overall, the family was in pretty good health. Even our dog, Buttercup, was feeling fine chasing local quail and the like. Life was good. And although pediatricians often gave my mother grief due to my extremely slender state, we never went hungry.

Truth be told, lots of great things happened during this period of my life. I learned to walk, figured out how to flush broccoli down the toilet, and even lost my first baby tooth! I couldn't have been any older than six when one day, while eating ice cream, I lost that first tooth. And by "lost," I mean *lost*. I knew the tooth was gone for good because my vanilla ice cream suddenly featured cherry-colored syrup and a solitary nut which I promptly swallowed. About a year or so later, after I had become an experienced tooth-loser, I woke up the morning after having lost another, and found two shiny quarters under my pillow. That's right, kids, fifty cents! *Ahhh*, I thought, *the legendary tooth fairy has paid me another visit.*

At this point in my young life, I wasn't all that sure about the tooth fairy. My parents would giggle suspiciously whenever I brought her up. On top of that, I was a pretty light sleeper and assumed I would wake up easily if some little Tinkerbell critter tried to drop a couple of coins under my pillow. Also, I knew other kids on the block who got like five dollars, some ten, and this one guy who, living only two doors down across the street, would get *twenty dollars* every time he lost a tooth! That's 400 dollars in his pocket by the time he'd lost all of his baby teeth, enough for a brand-new mid-2000s Lego Death Star! The Lego Death Star with like 4000 pieces! It just didn't make sense to me. *I'll have ten dollars and Nathan will have the coolest Lego set ever?!* I thought to myself. I didn't find Tinkerbell's system to be all that fair.

I woke up one morning, after having lost yet another tooth, and discovered, once again, two quarters under my pillow. Fifty cents could have gotten me a couple of sticks of bubblegum or perhaps a nice bouncy ball, so that was cool. But I already had a bouncy ball, and my mom usually had gum in her purse. Instead of making a quick purchase, I started to think about what else I might want. And it wasn't all that long until I had come up with my most desired desire: I wanted to find out if the tooth fairy was some great hoax put on by my mother. Perhaps it was a fib she had cooked-up along with a couple of other parents in the neighborhood.

I was homeschooled at the time and, since I was at home all day every day, knew my house pretty well. Thankfully, when I woke up that morning, I hadn't forgotten anything about the layout and confidently pranced out of the bedroom and into the living room where my mother's money jar was kept high on the top shelf of a bookcase. Making sure I had her attention from where she stood in the kitchen, I scooted a chair over to the bookcase and, with my two quarters in hand, stood on it reaching upward for the jar full of coins. From my tiptoes I grabbed the jar and opened it, plopping the money I had just received inside. As I did this, I looked my mother straight in the eyes and said with somewhat of a devious smile, "Mom, you didn't have to give those to me, I know money is tight right now."

To which she replied, "Oh, don't worry about it, sweetie—we have enough! Keep them!"

I had her.

I could see the blood draining from her face. I knew she had made up that whole tooth fairy thing and was in cahoots with, who knows, maybe like five or six other moms in the neighborhood. I had just Sherlocked my way into disrupting a local crime ring.

What can I say, after such a successful sleuth, life was going great. But then, as always seems to happen when things are going right, adversity struck. My mom started to get really sick. Like really, *really* sick. It turns out that she had endometriosis, which had plagued her for several years while doctors insisted that it was "all in her head" prior to her diagnosis. My sister, Kate, and I were home with Mom all day while Dad was at work. It seemed as though each day her health grew worse and worse. I remember her crawling along the floor, dressed in pajamas, scooting an old plastic butter container along with her just in case she needed to throw up, so as to get from one room to the other. As a kid, it began to feel normal having my mother in this constant state of fatigue. Hospital visits were commonplace. And late-night ambulance rides were a recurring phenomenon.

I did my best to emotionally detach myself from her during those years for fear that she would soon die. I even told some of my friends that the doctor had said she wouldn't even live another year or two. I guess I thought it would make things easier. Everybody grieves differently—I suppose I was just trying to grieve ahead of time. Whatever it was, it sucked. And on top of this, I wasn't sure what my role was in the family: Caregiver to my mom? Teacher to my homeschooled sister and my homeschooled self? Dog poo picker-upper? I didn't really know.

What I did know is that I didn't feel wanted and instead felt confused and conflicted. As such, my personal confusions with life were taken out on just about everything else as I became extremely obsessive: "The Freemasons are conspiring to take over the world!" "Gas prices are outrageous!"[24] "The FBI is attempting to contact me!" "I know where the Ark of the Covenant is!"[25] I was addicted to the adrenaline of my imagined reality. And as time went on, the addiction for attention, for validation, grew increasingly stronger.

This is the stage of my life where smelling "ceased." The stage where I printed out documents from the "CIA" to hide conspicuously in my bedroom, hoping someone would come across them and subsequently find me to be important. The stage where I bashed my ankle against the corner of my bunk bed, enduring the pain, in hopes of getting someone to take a moment out of their day to look my way and notice me. The stage where I boldface lied to people, vehemently claiming that I had met the President and been given a medal for valor (which I had actually picked up at a local pawn shop).

I was so desperate to be known. I wanted to be greater than I was. I so desperately wanted to be *Niq,* and not just Niq.

---

24 This right after Hurricane Katrina decimated Louisiana in August of 2005.

25 My bet is still on Axum, Ethiopia because, well, why not?

Even now, as I write this book more than a decade later, I question my intentions. Am I just writing to boost my own ego? To further my own wellbeing? To make Niq feel good about Niq? To be seen? To be validated? Am I writing this book because I want "me" to get somewhere? If I'm being honest, right now, I'm not sure I have a good answer for those questions. But what I am sure of is this: when we as humans strive to validate ourselves, perhaps by gaining an education or some advanced degree, a better title or higher position, or maybe just by working out in the gym five days a week, I don't think it directly helps with what we are tasked with as divine image-bearers. Which is, simply put, to act on the greatest commandment so as to carry out the great commission. When we strive to validate ourselves it does not help with our loving God by loving God's body. All this does is assist in "Niq feeling good about Niq," or "Lynda feeling good about Lynda," or "Sean feeling good about Sean." You get the idea.

But if I'm going to be honest with you, there has to be some kind of conscious movement away from this need for self-validation. I hear some of you groaning. It feels good to get that promotion after you sucked up to your boss. It feels good to take that family vacation after you've saved enough money. It feels good to walk down that graduation aisle after you've worked so hard to get through it all. It feels good to finally get that book published after you've worked so many countless hours on it. These are all great things, don't get me wrong—I suppose it's just our intent that matters.

The problem is that, at least from what I've learned, many of us are looking for validation in the wrong place. And I'll be honest with you here, I struggle with this every single day. Getting my dad to stumble across a secret "CIA" folder in my bedroom never magically did away with my need for validation, in the exact same way that going to church each weekend doesn't somehow make you any better than someone who stays home to watch a football game.

I know I'm not alone in feeling this way. Actually, dare I say, I'm in pretty good company because David, the guy who God says has God's heart, tells us to calm down and just live life without the burden of self-validation in one of his psalms:

> Commit your way to the Lord; trust in him, and he will act. He will make your vindication shine like the light, and the justice of your cause like the noonday. Be still before the Lord, and wait patiently for him; do not fret over those who prosper in their way, over those who carry out evil devices. Refrain from anger, and forsake wrath. Do not fret—it leads only to evil. For the wicked shall be cut off, but those who wait for the Lord shall inherit the land.[26]

David (yes, the same David who had a guy murdered just to rape his wife, so maybe I'm not in all that good of company) is keying us into the fact that God is the one who validates us—God provides us with God's stamp of approval which is the only stamp we really need! As I got older, I wish I had known this truth because, although my schemes for validation became less extravagant, they didn't stop. I tried to be seen as funny by friends and family, so I'd do things like run the local 5k backwards. I also turned to pornography, which, little did I know, would haunt and taunt me for the better part of a decade. These and my many other attempts at getting Niq to validate Niq backfired and usually ended up making me feel less-than. Maybe because I was looking for validation in the wrong place: I wanted Niq to validate Niq.

Now, if we're being honest with ourselves, we all need validation in some way or another. We all want to hear that we are greater than we know ourselves to be. We all do and say the stupidest things in hopes of feeling like we matter. And while this line from John is so

---

26 Psalm 37:5-9.

cliche, it's cliche for a reason. The same reason, I think, that persuaded David to write that psalm. Perhaps because it's true: "For God so loved the cosmos as to *give* the Son, the only one."[27] It's a truth further articulated by Tom Wright when he says that, "God's great future purpose was not to rescue people out of the world, but to rescue the world itself, people included, from its present state of disruption and decay."[28] This act of divine rescue is the very heart of the gospel.[29] And if a rescue mission for all of humanity—yourself included—doesn't sound like validation, on a universal and yet so intimate scale, I don't know what is.

Jesus as the gift of a God who only loves and love as the validation we all so desperately desire. Because God is only love. Love itself is God.

Hearing that, some may want to call me an atheist because their version of theism exists squarely within three dimensions as they cling only to a visible, touchable, imaginable God—often an old white man living amongst the clouds above. Yet my version of theism exists beyond the fourth dimension of time and moves into a fifth, similarly nonvisualized, unimaginable dimension of love, grace, and goodness. A dimension not seen but lived in and through. Of course, my perspective, a perspective I think scripture supports, could seem atheistic to some. For we would not believe in the same God. However, the reason I readily push back on the traditional view of God here in this work is because when we see our God as one who perpetrates systems of oppression, when our God is violent, and if our God is anything but wholly good, that God is not worth thinking on.[30] "If the concept

---

27 John 3:16. Emphasis added.

28 N.T. Wright, *How God Became King*, 45.

29 See Stanely Grenz, *Renewing the Center*, 345.

30 Philippians 4:8.

of God has any validity or any use," wrote James Baldwin, "it can only be to make us larger, freer, and more loving. If God cannot do this, then it is time we got rid of him."[31]

Harmful portraits of God often gravitate around white patriarchal systems, initially propagated by European colonization and more recently Christian nationalism, which subsequently exist as justification for deplorable acts to take place in the name of such a deity.[32] Yet, when a portrait of God does no harm, when our God is seen as pacifistic (more on that in a coming chapter), it is then helpful in that our perceiving of God in this way can act as a catalyst for creating more of Godself—love, grace, and goodness. For, if we are honest, God presents Godself to us all in different ways. Atheists and Buddhists are not juxtaposed, but both possess the divine love in variant forms. Christian and Muslim expressions are not contrasts of one another, instead their understandings of God are both incomplete yet vital parts of the beautiful mosaic that is love.

This is why conversion-minded and evangelistic religious expressions, which can seem holy and good in the moment, often grow into Godzilla-like monsters that become untamed agents of destruction. For in them we have chosen doctrine and thought over practice and being. But it is clear God does not task us to convert. Instead we're tasked to love—to make lovers of all nations. If John's recollection tells us anything it's that the rescue has happened—past tense—as in you've already been rescued, you're already in. Love has cleaned you and will clean you again. So, just be. Be who you were created to be. Be *you*.

Because you are who God loves unconditionally, no matter what.

---

31 James Baldwin, "Letter from a Region in My Mind," *The New Yorker*.

32 See Kristin Du Mez, *Jesus and John Wayne*, 301.

4

THE "F" WORD

Love can be a strange thing. Sometimes when we couldn't imagine any being left in our tanks, there is more. Even after my mother was tricked into telling me that the tooth fairy was indeed a hoax, after recovering from several illnesses which had plagued her, and after greiving a devastating miscarriage, she and my father decided they still had more love to give. Together, they ended up exploring the idea of fostering children in transition from their biological homes to that of a more permanent foster care situation.

I remember sitting in our living room one winter as our family's case counselor from Child Protective Services went through loads and loads of paperwork with my parents. She must have been in her thirties, with short blonde hair, and a distinct walk. She would ask scenario questions like: "What would you do if your foster child swallowed a Lego?" or, "Do you see yourself as someone with a lot of emotional energy?" Sometimes my sister, Kate, and I had to leave the room because they were talking about sensitive *adult* stuff, but we would usually just go close one of our bedroom doors, loud enough to be sure all of the adults would have heard it, then sneak back towards the living room to listen in on the conversation. Eventually, after months of training and background checks, everything had been cleared, and I was ready for the little brother I had always wanted but never gotten. It was going to be incredible!

It was early summer by the time we got the call we had long been anticipating. We were finally going to foster a kid! Actually, we were going to foster *kids*. That's right, folks! Not only was I going to get that long-awaited brother, but his twin sister as well! To our knowledge, we were going to host them no more than a month before they were placed into a more permanent situation. We hurried to gather age-appropriate clothes and toiletries, you know, like miniature socks and toothbrushes, and waited eagerly for their arrival.

They arrived on our front porch in the evening, one clutching a small blanket, the other an empty bottle of water quite obviously provided by their transport. They both seemed timid, quiet, and scared. This was not at all what I had envisioned. I suppose that I half-expected them to come riding in on a unicorn or something, triumphantly, with a wink and a nod. Bearing gifts perhaps, like a couple of mini Christmas magi! But that was quite obviously not the case. In fact, much of what I had imagined about my new siblings, J and Shayla, turned out to be just that, *imagined*.[33]

Having been raised in a homeschool environment, my only real connection to the horrors of the world outside of the bubble in which I lived were my treasured history books. Even then, I did not seem to have the mental capacity to make connections between the terrors of Nazi Germany and the exploits of the United States in their genocidal conquest of Native Americans. I picked sides. And I always, subconsciously, picked the side of the "winner" (or at least who I was told had won). It was into this mindset that J and Shayla stepped. And they forever turned my world upside down.

---

33 With the exception of those who have given permission for the use of their names in this book, many names and, at times, circumstances have been altered to preserve anonymity.

The first thing my mother did when the twins arrived was to get them bathed and have their clothes washed. I was clear across at the other end of the house, helping my dad prepare some dinner, when I heard shrieks of terror coming from the bathroom. As it turns out, Mom had drawn up a nice warm bath for the two nearly three year-olds and, the moment the water touched them, they began to scream and cry in what seemed to be utter pain. As we later learned, the home they had just come from didn't have hot water, and so their bodies were used to nothing more than cold. The warm water burned. Though I didn't know how to verbalize it at the time, this was the moment I first became conscious of my privilege.

J didn't move into my bedroom as I had anticipated but instead stayed with Shayla in what used to be my parents' study. I had kind of wanted J to move into my room and sleep on the bottom bunk. Maybe he would want to help redecorate the room as I transitioned out of my lengthy space-craze (to be honest, it's not really over; I'm still obsessed). Out with the planetarium, in with baseball perhaps? Sadly, without him sharing the room, the anticipated redecorating didn't happen.

Having been so sheltered all of my life, weekend church services were my only real social outlet. That being said, the fundamentalist ideals which seemed so appealing in their presentation, frequently kept my head busy throughout the night. Often, I didn't feel anything from God but shame and reproach; yet, for some reason, I felt as though I had to fake a joyous relationship with Jesus because that's what "saved" people did. And I sure as the hot place didn't want to end up in the hot place, so I played the part as best as I could.

I had never actually heard the "f" word before J and Shayla came into our lives and, as such, didn't recognize it's profanity. My mother, bless her, was convinced the twins were demon-possessed at times. They would throw the most horrific tantrums; screaming, swearing, spitting, and spewing. And the kids weren't yet three! She would pray over them, as a prayer was about all she could muster. Eventually, she gained permission from our CPS case counselor to strap them into their car seats, set inside the living room, so as to restrain them during the "possessions."

I didn't understand it. I had no context with which to empathize. I had never been sexually assaulted. Never gone starving. Never been beaten by those who were to take care of me. Never neglected as my parents got hyped-up on drugs. J and Shayla had seen more in their three years of life than I could have ever imagined; my seeing it second-hand blew my world way out of the water. For it was during the twins' "two to four week stay" with us, as promised by CPS, which ended up being over a year-and-a-half, that the bubble my parents had created in an attempt to shelter me from the reality of life began to burst.

My dad had, as aforementioned, been professionally trained as a mortician. And from what he tells me, he liked it. I'm sure he was great with the dead bodies and all, but he quit his apprenticeship around the time I was born. Since then he has worked in transportation, healthcare, senior living, education, construction, social services, and, at the time the twins came into our lives, as the manager of a local Christian radio station. Being the kid of a radio station's manager in a mid-size town has its perks. I got to hear myself on-air voicing commercials, and Dad got free vocal talent. I also got into pretty much any local concert or event for free. And, at those concerts and events, I would get all of the free stickers, pens, lanyards, and mints that I wanted from other sponsoring stations or businesses in the community. So yeah, being a station manager's kid had it perks for sure.

One particular day, Dad and I went to a hunting convention. Now I'm not sure how he had gotten his Christian music station, targeted at soccer moms in their thirties and forties, a booth at that particular event. Maybe we just went because he likes guns. I don't know. Anyhow, as we walked in, there was a raffle bucket where you could leave your ticket stub with your name written on it, in hopes of winning a raffle prize. There were lots of prizes, and, if I remember correctly, the grand prize was a hunting bow. I could have cared less about the bow, however, as my eyes were focused on several gift certificates for large pizzas at Papa John's. Truth be told, we Ruuds were Papa Murphy's people, but free pizza is free pizza. You've got to take what you can get! So although the drawings hadn't even started yet, with the possibility of free pizza, I was ecstatic.

As the evening wore on, this burly cowboy would periodically point to a kid out in the crowd and bring them onstage to draw a ticket stub out from the bucket once kept by the door. He was a tall man, black felt cowboy hat, blue jeans, brown jacket—like a Carhartt model. I remember, too, how distinctly he held the microphone— with the tip gently resting in the soul patch on his chin. It looked cool. He looked cool.

While I was sitting there in the crowd, the cool cowboy pointed in my direction. So I got up, climbed onto the stage over to his left, and drew a name out of the bucket. He rested the mic to my mouth, just below my lips, the cool way, and I opened it to read *my name*. Suddenly, as I'm sure you would have been, I was smiling ear to ear. I looked up at the cowboy who had returned the mic to his soul patch and raised my hand in victory. He didn't seem to notice me and instead was yelling out into the crowd, "Niq Ruud, is there a Niq Ruud here? Niq Ruud with a funny spelling? With a 'Q'? Niq Ruud?" Eventually, he looked below at the little kid jumping up and down beside his knees and realized that I must indeed be this "Niq Ruud" fella he'd been hollering for. I went home that night as the proud owner of a gift certificate for free pizza, which, much to my chagrin, Dad made me share with the rest of the family. Yet eating that pizza was maybe the happiest I ever saw J and Shayla. They smiled from ear to ear, just as I had when I found out that I had drawn my own name out of the free pizza bucket.

It's been over a decade since my family has heard anything about or from the twins. As delusional as I might be to say that I saw love in those two bundles of absolute insanity, I most certainly did. J may have been the most sincere person I've ever met, even at just three years old. He wore his emotions on his sleeve and always wanted the best for those he loved most. And while Shayla was deeply hurt by her past circumstances and, consequently, the most willing to manipulate those around her so as to avoid a repeat of such pain, I saw in her an unwavering love for her brother, who she would do anything to protect.

That's the exact kind of love Jesus is portrayed as displaying in scripture. God subjects Godself to humanity, God becomes man, a man on a mission—with the distinct directive of showing us what unwavering and ever-faithful love looks like in a wavering and unfaithful world.[34] Personally, I think Jesus did a pretty good job of it. His sincerity persuaded thousands. His cunning circumvented many more in their attempts to thwart his mission. But he kept pushing on,

---

34 I often use "leveled" language in this book for the sake of readability. Such verbiage does not fully reflect my thoughts on the matter which have been heavily influenced by the likes of Diana Butler Bass, particularly in her book, *Grounded*.

fighting to change the way humans understood their creator. Not as a god of shame and guilt, but instead a God of love. *Only love.*

And let me be honest here for a second, that kind of god, the one which is always looking at us from over our shoulders, trying to catch us in the act, that god is a *human* conceptualization. That version of god is not real. But for some reason many of us who grew up in Christians circles cling to this particular god like it's the only god available. The problem is that throughout the Bible we read that God, the real God, is a God of mercy, grace, and love from the very beginning![35] Perhaps too many pastors and priests have twisted those three words, intertwining shame into their meanings, allowing guilt and love to marry. But God is not a god of fear.[36] In fact, we see, through the humanity of Jesus, a God who despises fear. Let me share an example with you.

Jesus, as you probably already know, was really into magic tricks. He wasn't all that into playing cards or disappearing rabbits, but is presented by the gospel writers to have been keen on tricks that had to do with liquid. Like fish, wine, and, well, water. One day he decides to take a hike, on the water, and his pals kind of freak out. They think that Jesus is a ghost and cry out in fear. But we're told that Jesus immediately said to them: "Take heart, it is I; do not be afraid."[37]

Jesus wasn't into fear. Neither is God. You see, the disciples' understanding of Jesus in that moment was shrouded in what they had already presupposed. They had seen Jesus, yes, but *saw* a ghost and, perhaps rightfully, freaked the heck out! They had seen God, yes, but *saw* something else entirely. I think a lot of us are like the disciples

---

35 Exodus 34:6-7.

36 Abraham Joshua Heschel, *The Prophets*, 391.

37 Matthew 14:27.

on that boat and we see a ghost when we're looking at God, especially if we've gone digging around some often brushed over places in the Bible. Because, more often than not, that god, if taken at face value, is a god that *loves*, sure, but loves through *fear*. And most of us probably want to quit believing in a god who controls us through fear, but it's hard to look through the mess of human bias and find the truth of God's character behind it. It's almost as though we see a ghost, a ghost that's not at all what we really *see*.

Yet, because the love of God expressed in Jesus is so unwavering, so steady, so much like the love J and Shayla had for each other, perhaps it's simply the human perception of the divine, both of the historical authors and the readers of their work, that has caused us to fear. If we're going to take seriously the personality of Jesus, perhaps we'll come to recognize that what we've been taught to see in God, the bad, may not be real at all—and that God is nothing more than unwavering love. I really like what the author David Hansen says about this God: "There is nothing inside God but God—even the love of God within God is God."[38] Most views of god are narrow like the beam of a flashlight at midnight, illuminating only what it is pointed at. Yet, love reveals all as the light of the sun at noon. It transcends the light of the flashlight, yet includes what it, too, reveals. Hansen seems to get that flashlights are worthless at noon—that with a larger, all encompassing light, our flashlights are worthless. That even the love of God *is God*.

I'd gone so far as to say that the holy love conveyed between us humans is God. Flowing in and through us all. It's a love deeper than mine for pizza. A love deeper than J and Shayla for each other. A love deeper than anything imaginable as there are no strings attached. Because God is a love that's f***ing awesome.

---

38 David Hansen, *The Art of Pastoring*, 47.

5

OFFICER K

I've been blessed to have many friends over the years whose love towards me has been f***ing awesome. During my early years in college, some of these friends and I did these things called "Rooks Runs." We would start across town at Rooks Park and, long after the sun had set, ride longboards, bikes, scooters, and roller skates the ten or so kilometers back to our university's campus. It was mostly downhill, so we could easily chat with one another as we went along. No heavy breathing or anything—it was always a great time.

Now, while a longboard was easily the traditional choice of transportation for our trips, I didn't own one. And, with my childhood days of neighborhood scooter Olympics long behind me, I didn't own a scooter either. I did have a pair of rollerblades, but, well, they were for roller hockey, and I wanted to keep their wheels in tip-top condition. So, for most of our Rooks Runs, I rode my bike.

I liked my bike. It cost me exactly zero dollars. This, thanks to my dad who, while driving a bus for work, had been gifted it from someone who didn't want to fix its flat tire. As I knew how to fix a flat, Dad donated it to me. And as soon as it was in my possession I was riding all over the place. From the dorm to the cafeteria. From the cafeteria to work. From work to class. From class to class. And even from work to work! It was a great little bike. Sadly, the bike wasn't as happy to have me around as I was to have it, and so, one afternoon before a scheduled Rooks Run, it decided to go and get itself stolen.

Now to be clear, this wasn't going to be just any Rooks Run, this was an end of the quarter Rooks Run! *Very special!* The whole crew was getting together and I couldn't miss it!

Since my bike had so recently chosen to end our relationship, I started making the rounds. I went all over the place looking for someone to lend me a transportation device. I went to my roommate. I went to my next-door neighbor. I went to the dormitory dean. I went to my boss' house (his wife answered the door and was pretty confused). I even went to the school library, but they had some dumb policy about only lending out books.

So later that night, I arrived, empty-handed, at my friend's house situated just behind campus. At least fifteen people had gathered, ready for a brilliant nocturnal adventure. School was out for spring break, and we were all ready to celebrate by slowly traveling ten kilometers in the dark! One of the people present in the house that evening was my friend, Hope. Now, Hope is a great gal. She has this whole hippie vibe about her: long braided hair, bright and colorful clothes, unconventional shoes, and, most importantly, a really cool van. It was this sweet 1970s Dodge with an intricately hand-painted landscape mural for the interior. Super cool. On top of her rad ride, Hope is a generous soul—that evening, when she realized I had walked into the house empty-handed, Hope offered me her longboard, saying she was planning to roller skate this particular Rooks Run anyway.

We all had a great time that night. Especially me. Because, well, it was my very first time on a longboard. About halfway back to campus I just about got hit by a white sedan who had made a blind left-hand turn, across the bike lane I was longboarding in, towards the other side of the road. I leapt off of the longboard, falling on my butt, and watched as the borrowed board slid perfectly between the four wheels of the car, exiting on the other side without so much as a scratch.

Believe it or not, that was actually the only fall I had all night! Again, it was my first time longboarding. *Be impressed, people!*

We arrived back to campus just after midnight. And with no school in the morning, nor for the next week and a half of mornings, along with a hungry tummy after my near-death experience, I decided I wanted Taco Bell. And, you guessed it, I wanted Taco Bell right then and there. Luckily, Hope did too. So, we tossed our wheels into the back of her little commuter truck (which was not as cool a rig as her artsy van but did get better gas mileage) and set our course due east for the land of bell-shaped tacos.

I don't remember what I ordered that night, but I do remember that after eating, Hope and I each put one of her roller skates on and took turns long-skating (yes, we invented a new sport) around a nearby parking lot. One foot on the longboard and another in a roller skate. It was actually pretty fun. You should try it late one night after your exam week is finished.

It was nearing 1:30 a.m. when we turned Hope's truck back towards campus. And we had made it within a stone's throw of my dorm room before I became distracted by something on the sidewalk. It was small. It was fluffy. And it was unmistakably a cat!

Now, for those of you who don't know, I love cats. I love dogs more, yes, but I love cats a whole heck of a lot, too. Like I would be totally content and happy if the only creatures on the planet were cats (and us humans, of course). I had this cat as a kid; her name was Sugar because she was pretty sweet. I got her when she was just a tiny little thing, and at night I would have her sleep on her back in the crook of my arm. She would purr really loud for hours on end, it was so cute! During her waking moments, she would come, kind of like a dog, when I did this weird call with my lips. Sugar even played fetch with a little fuzzball toy! She was probably as close to a dog as a cat ever could be. I loved it!

But there I was, riding shotgun in Hope's truck. We had time to kill, it was spring break, and I had seen a cat! Now, to be fair, although Sugar was long gone, all cats look like Sugar in the dark. I asked Hope to stop. She likes cats, too, so she pulled off to the side of the road. I stepped out of the truck and, with a skate still on my left foot, skate-walked over towards the cute and cuddly fluffball sitting on the sidewalk.

Once I was within a meter or so, I started doing that weird lip call that I always did with Sugar. (I figured it might be some universal cat thing.) This new fluffy friend of mine didn't seem to find the call quite as attractive as Sugar once had, and so he scooted himself just across the property line—from public concrete to private front yard grass. Now, I'm not one to give up easily, so I started calling a little bit louder, hoping he would respond by letting me pet him for a moment or two. Sadly, he didn't. But, in a way, the call I made actually worked because *someone* heard it.

As I was squatting on the sidewalk, a singular skate still firmly attached to my left foot, several hours after midnight, sporting a rambunctiously long and unkempt head of hair, I heard a familiar wisp of air on the road behind me. It was a quiet vehicle, not electric, but very high-tech. I knew it wasn't Hope's truck; she was parked and I would have heard her turn on the engine. I knew it wasn't my car because, well, my car was loud and dying, and I had the keys in my pocket. After the wisp of air passed behind me, it slowed down and then, just as I turned my head over my left shoulder to check it out, it dawned on me that this vehicle belonged to our town's local police force.

I didn't move. Thinking that perhaps if I held myself still enough, they would just think I was a two-legged, one-skate bump in the sidewalk. Sadly, my tactic didn't work. After turning around near the end of the street, the squad car slowed down as it passed me for a second time. Then, from inside the cab, I heard the unmistakable sound of a police radio. My heart sank. *Is this really how I'll end up in prison?* I thought.

As suspicious as I thought I looked, I soon realized that the squad car was leaving. It had whisked itself right away! I turned my head to the right and saw it taking a left at a stop sign about the length of a football pitch or so to the north. Relieved, I quickly stood up, said goodbye to my new kitty friend, and skate-walked as fast as I could back to Hope, still sitting in her truck. She had the engine started before I could even skate-hop inside. We exchanged glances of relief and were off without so much as a word.

On second thought, language like, "we were off" is actually pretty misleading. Because we had gone no more than a stone's throw down the road before those unmistakable red and blue lights were alit behind us. Hope pulled over, put her keys on the dash, her hands on the wheel, and rolled down her driver's side window.

Moments later, an officer appeared at her door and began asking us questions as to what we were doing. Truthfully, I don't remember the exact verbiage he used, primarily because I was so enamored by the name tag on his bulletproof vest: Officer K.

Officer K was somewhat of a famous figure around campus. Or I should say, *infamous*. I'd had several run-ins with this particular cop prior to that late night, none of which I particularly enjoyed. One afternoon, I was riding my bike back to my dorm room from a work meeting only a kilometer from campus. It was raining and I didn't have a rain jacket with me. So naturally, I held my vest up above my head as an umbrella. Moments later, Officer K pulled me over for "riding my bike without holding onto the handlebars." A few months prior, one night while on a run, he "pulled me over" and threatened to cuff me if I didn't go back to campus right away (there was no local curfew in effect for those of you wondering). And these were just my experiences! Peers, professors, and friends all had their own Officer K stories to share, many of which far worse than mine as they involved firearms coupled with clueless citizens.

As strange as all this may have been, perhaps the strangest thing about Officer K was that he never seemed to recognize anybody. My freshman year, I worked in a restaurant just north of campus. Every Wednesday, every week, without fail, Officer K would come into the restaurant, ask for a sample of our potato salad, then order some to-go. At first I didn't think twice, but eventually, after enough weekly requests, I was like, *What? Why does he need to sample it every week?* I mean come on, he knew what it tasted like! I would frequently run into him at the grocery store, too. But even with all of our various interactions, both personal and professional, he never waved, he never said hello, and he never smiled.

It seemed like he was dead inside.

As soon as I realized it was Officer K who had pulled us over, my heart sank even further. While I don't remember the exact words he used, he questioned Hope and I as to what we were doing and why we were doing it. I only remember responding to his questions with, "Well, I just wanted to pet the cat." He seemed worried that I might have crossed a property line and trespassed. I worried that he might think I was a catnapper!

I retold this story a lot in the dorm over the next couple of years, it seemed to really get a crowd going. Full disclosure … I don't know if this part of the story actually happened or if it is just a figment of my imagination, but I think Officer K had me get out of Hope's truck and walk a line. He thought I was drunk. So I got out of the truck, skate still firmly attached to my left foot, and asked the police officer, who was notorious for, at times, pulling his gun on innocent, unarmed citizens, if he wanted me to hop the line on one foot or skate it on the other. If my memory serves me correctly, he said he didn't care, and so I skated the most perfect and prettiest line you've ever seen, turned around, and skated right back to the starting point!

What I remember for sure is that Officer K took both our licenses, along with Hope's vehicle insurance and registration, back to his squad car. It was way past either of our bedtimes at this point, and all I could think about was getting back to my dorm room and going to sleep! A few minutes later, Officer K came back, returned our paperwork, angrily told us to stay off the streets, then retreated back to his car.

Hope quickly started her truck's engine and pulled back into the road. As she drove us away, I turned around to look at Officer K's squad car which had been parked behind us. It was then that I noticed two or three other police cars, red and blue lights ablaze, parked behind Officer K's. We were flabbergasted! Enraged, even, that my wanting to pet a cat had taken a handful of cars worth of taxpayer dollars to enforce!

In hindsight, if this experience taught me anything it is that while Officer K didn't need to call for backup, and while it most certainly was a waste of taxpayer money, this minute injustice pales in comparison to what my siblings of various minorities go through in Western society each and every day. Friends, I write this chapter in the summer of 2020—the Covid-19 pandemic rages; politics have divided my country; many of us are fed up with the injustices we see all around. So, while this is not a central theme of *Only Love*, I must contend that all lives do not matter until Black, Asian, Native, Latinx, LGBTQIA+, poor, disabled, and every other marginalized life is treated and affirmed as if it does. I'm not saying the change will come easy—in fact, if history has taught us anything, it will be very hard—but until the day in which all people are treated as the image-bearers of God that they are, we have failed to only love.

After my experience that evening, my heart grew cold towards Officer K. Every time I saw him in the supermarket, I didn't smile in his direction as I had before. Instead, I gave him *the look*. Every time he came into the restaurant looking for a taste of potato salad, I gave him half as much of a sample as I used to. The problem was I became so afraid of what Officer K might do to me that I never thought of what I might be able to do for him. He seemed oppressive. Heck, he was oppressive! He seemed to hate college kids like me, and maybe he did. But I had the opportunity to love him right through it all, and I blew it. I blew it really badly.

I know that a lot of the stories I've shared so far have been about times when I've seen love. Times when I've felt love. And, yes, even those times when I've smelled it. But this story is strikingly different as it is about a time when I chose hate. It's a story where I intentionally chose not to love. Where I did what felt right in the moment and lost sight of greater things.

If I'm honest with myself, this is just one story out of thousands which I could offer as an example of what not to do. And it's a pretty soft one at that. I can be, and have been, a really terrible person when the right moment comes along. And while I'm saddened by my inability to only love all of the time, it reminds me of the one who is said to have come in our stead so that we wouldn't have to be haunted by our shortcomings—when the God who created the universe subjected Godself to a created body just like yours and mine. When Jesus, God in the flesh, was bound by human restrictions like gender, culture, time, and religious creed. This individual, this being, this God went from infinite to finite, subjecting Godself to the most oppressive practices known to humanity to show us that we're living in the storyline of the greatest party in the history of the universe. Or, as Paul said, where God is all in all.[39] A place where love will be everything.

It's not like God's choice to become us all, in the person of Jesus, was somehow made assuming it would be easy, because God became human. Honestly, I don't know how else to say this, but *God became human*. Love, formless and infinite, entered into solidarity with the formed and finite. "God's eternal nature," says Greg Boyd, "is the kind of love that is willing to set aside the blessedness and privileges of being God, stooping to unite Godself with our humanity, and then stooping even further to unite Godself with our sin and our God-forsaken curse."[40] *Love became human.*

Check out this moment in a garden just outside of the ancient city of Jerusalem. Empathize with the uncertainty of the love-human Jesus' future. This being who knew no limit in cognitive capacity who had chosen to step into the unknown of finiteness.[41] Empathize with the fear of his not now knowing what would transpire:

> Then Jesus ... says to the disciples, "Sit down here while I go apart in order to pray over there." And, taking along Peter and the sons of Zebedee, he began to grieve and suffer distress. Then he says to them, "My soul is in anguish, to the point of death; remain here and keep watch with me."[42]

Luke, too, records the event saying that Jesus' "sweat became like drops of blood falling to the earth."[43] The humanity demonstrated in these and other verses, show us the incredible willingness of God

---

1 Corinthians 15:28.

40 Greg Boyd, *Inspired Imperfection*, 89.

41 Psalm 147:5; Hebrews 4:13; Job 37:16.

42 Matthew 26:36-38.

43 Luke 22:44.

to love even those who we humans would peg as being the worst. It demonstrates the kind of God that loves Officer K just as much as God loves your sister or favorite uncle. A God that loves Adolf Hitler just as much as God loves Mother Theresa or Martin Luther King Jr. Because with this self-sacrificial, only loving God, it doesn't matter how terrible you think you are, or how great people tell you that you may be, somehow we're all tied for first in the eyes of love.[44]

I know, infinite love doesn't make intuitive sense. Colonized Christianity has programmed many of us to think that good things are supposed to happen to good people and that justice operates in God's kingdom the same way as it does in our judicial system—where those who break the law, or to use biblical language, "sin," are subject to retributive punishment. But instead, biblical justice appears restorative—where people who screw things up, even intentionally, are restored in love. It's utterly counterintuitive. It doesn't make sense that God might love you, a genuinely good person I'm sure, as much as God loves that terribly, terrible coworker or neighbor or spouse of yours. But God does. I see good reason to believe that even scripture points to the kind of God that is in the business of loving the people who are hardest to love. Because God is love.

A love that loves all—the worst of the worst included.

Even you.

Even me.

---

44 Paraphrased from Bob Goff, *Everybody, Always*, ix.

6

A POOPY CHRISTMAS

But how could God love us if we're so dirty and broken? The worst of the worst? And I mean, in a way, we all kind of are because sometimes life can get dirty—like really, really dirty. As a kid, things usually got kind of gross in the middle of summer with sweat from the heat and mud from our family's little strawberry patch. But it wasn't all that often that things got dirty come wintertime. There was snow on the ground and the sun was usually hiding back behind some clouds. No sweat, no mud. Things never got gross. And because of that, for me, as for many small children, Christmas, honestly, was "the most wonderful time of the year."

Our family would often gather at my grandparents' house in the small rodeo town of Pendleton, Oregon, where we would get the chance to eat tasty treats, sing classy Christmas carols, and most importantly, play with our favorite cousins. Christmas time in a rodeo town is pretty much like Christmas most anywhere else—you've got delightful lights up on porches, evergreen trees chopped down and then propped up in living rooms, not to mention the great smells coming from kitchens far and near.

This particular Christmas I must have been about eight or nine. As the oldest of all the cousins, I had first choice on which bed I would sleep in for the duration of the holiday. Wisely, and as all good eight-year-olds do, I picked the top bunk—a great place to spy on the younger cousins sleeping down below and an even better place to keep watch and be certain no one got kidnapped by Santa.

It was Christmas Eve, and although I had been potty-trained long ago, my ability to hold "it" through the night was still in a preliminary stage of development. I awoke, probably around one or two that morning, and quietly descended from my plush fortress so as to tiptoe across the hall to the basement's bathroom facility.

The small bathroom had no door and no hinges to hang one, had someone wanted to put a real barrier up. Instead, a seemingly ancient curtain rod sported an equally-ancient bedsheet which one could pull across the bare door frame for some semblance of privacy. Not wanting to wake my cousins, Andy and Ray, sleeping on the floor in the room across from me, which conveniently also lacked a proper door, I opted not to turn on the bathroom lights. Instead, I waved my hands around in the darkness until my fingertips brushed up against the familiar feel of a porcelain throne.

Lifting the seat cover I proceeded to sit, not stand, since I might have missed the toilet completely in the surrounding darkness, to complete my business. As I lowered myself onto the seat, I quickly noticed something where something should not have been. In the absence of air, there was water. Or, at least, something similar to it.

Standing up quickly, I turned around and fumbled for the flusher. I flushed, and for a moment all seemed as it should have. I heard the toilet flushing. I felt the reverberations of the toilet flushing. I even smelled the toilet flushing (as this was well before my life's great scientific study began). But low and behold, the toilet did not flush. Instead, I felt what should have been flushed down into the sewer begin to permeate the cotton barrier between me and my freshly Christmas-stockinged feet. Something was most certainly wrong.

First, I closed the bed sheet curtain (as a courtesy to my cousins) and turned on the light. Second, I began opening the cupboards above the washer and dryer adjacent to the toilet looking for towels to clean up the brown, gooey mess. Third, I flushed the toilet again, just in case it could somehow reverse the depressing outcome I was witnessing. Sadly, it did not.

I tried flushing again and again and again, but the chunky chocolate deluge continued. Now quite flustered, I began to try and dam the doorway leading into the hall with nearby towels and bedsheets, lying on the washer and dryer across from the chocolate fondue, so as to avoid the spread of this seemingly "natural" disaster. I don't remember screaming or making enough noise to wake anyone up, but maybe the constant flushing paralleled by the sound of the brown cascade, or the light shining through the thin sheet-curtain did the trick. Either way, my cousin Andy was the first to wake to the muddy flood. The mess had breached my dam and found its way across the hall to my holiday roommate's bed. And soon enough, after several screams of terror, footsteps could be heard upstairs. Lights were quickly turned on, and then the parents—all of them—arrived on the scene. I felt terrible: *If only I had just held it, none of this mess would have happened,* I thought.

Soon, the police showed up. Sorry, the plumbers. Soon, the *plumbers* showed up. It could have been the cops; I mean I felt as though I should have been in trouble for the chocolaty mess. The plumbers made their way downstairs to the little bathroom at what was probably four or five on that now dreadful Christmas morning. As it turned out, a pipe had frozen, cracked, and obviously unfroze just enough to vomit out an early Christmas present for my granddad's pocketbook.

I'm sure the mess was cleaned up eventually, but I didn't get to catch any more of the action as I was quickly ushered upstairs to take a shower in the one bathroom fancy enough to sport both hinges and a door! The room across from the upstairs bathroom was where my great-great-grandmother lived. Yes, you've read that right: great-*great*!

She was ninety-three or ninety-four years old at the time, something like that, and was bedridden—needing to be bathed by my grandmother (her granddaughter!) each day with a warm washcloth.

As I hopped into the shower to rid myself of the entire extended family's feces, I quickly grabbed the washcloth hanging up on the shower curtain rod where my mother always left one for me back at home. After several minutes of vigorously scrubbing my face, body, and feet I started to rinse off. Needless to say, I was feeling much better about my situation, but then came a knock at the door. "Niq? Can I come in?" my mother asked, "I've got a washcloth here for you."

To my horror, I had just scrubbed my face with my great-great-grandma's *used* bath cloth. I froze, unable to rid myself of the horrible sinking feeling wrenching my stomach. This Christmas could not have gotten any worse. I don't remember crying, but I am almost certain I did. The water, still streaming-down from above, must have covertly concealed my tears. Mom came in, took the now twice-used washcloth away, replaced it with a new one, and did her best to comfort me.

I scrubbed myself with that new washcloth harder than ever before. I wanted every cell of my skin to just die and flake off. To this day, I blame all of the acne I've ever had on that singular moment.

This is exactly what sin is like.

It's sitting there, pooling and festering, waiting to get us in the middle of the night. And far too often it does get us, even when it's not really our fault. Sometimes, we even wash ourselves with more of it thinking it will rid us of what we've already accumulated! Half of the time, we don't even realize it's bad for us; it disguises itself as something good. It's hanging there on the curtain rod! Just where the clean washcloth should be. David Bentley Hart writes that, "Everyone committing sin is a slave to sin ... and a slave, needless to say, is not free."[45] Meaning that sin is the inescapable reality of our being alive. It is a universal problem we all face. It is lodged inside of us.[46] We have lost our freedom, and we'll never really rid ourselves of such poop.

Paul is this guy who is said to have written a lot of correspondence to different people around the ancient Roman Empire. He used to be called "Saul" and is one of a whole host of people who get their name changed in the Bible. While he was still Saul, he was passionately and devoutly married to the ancient rules and traditions of the Hebrew religion. He was so passionate and so devout that he saw Jesus and his followers as a serious threat to his traditional way of life and was adamant on destroying the movement they had initiated. But then Saul had this crazy encounter with Jesus where his name swap happened. And with that swap came a great commission where Saul, now Paul, was convinced to take seriously the task of telling non-Jewish people about the love that God is.

Paul eventually writes a really interesting letter to some house churches in Rome which might be the closest thing we've got to a first-century textbook on cross-cultural ministry. Anyway, in this mini-textbook, Paul, who used to kill Christ-followers for their radical ideas, makes somewhat of a radical confession himself:

> I do not know what it is that I accomplish; because what I wish, this I do not do; instead, what I hate, this I do. But so long as I do not do this, what I wish, I am in agreement with the Law—that is good. But now no longer am I at work, but rather the sin that dwells within me. For I know that in me—that is, in my flesh—dwells nothing good; for it is present in me to will, but not to accomplish, the good; for I do not do the good

---

45 David Bentley Hart, *That All Shall Be Saved*, 80.

46 As characterized by Diane Langberg in, *Suffering and the Heart of God*, 39.

I wish; instead, the evil I do not wish, this I do. But if what I do not wish, this I do, then no longer am I operating, but rather the sin that dwells within me.[47]

My, do we have ourselves a philosopher here! But Paul seems to get it. He understands that poo is simply a part of life. A nasty, stinky, gross part of life, yes, but something that we can't go around beating ourselves up for. Paul understands that sin is the inescapable reality of our being alive, and that it is the universal problem we all face. And he, too, gets that we'll never really be able to rid ourselves of the poop.

Now, I don't mean to be a downer, but the poop has made it everywhere. It covers every centimeter of us all. You, just as much as me. That guy you hate down the street, just as much as the nice bank teller you always look forward to chatting with. And the poo is naughty, let's not sugar-coat it! It most certainly is not nice! I wish all of life were sugar plums and reindeer with bright red noses, but it's not. What we call sin makes life hard, and life really stinks sometimes. People cheat. Lie. Steal. Even kill. We create structures of oppression and pain. We forgive only ourselves and then turn around to condemn our neighbors. There is suffering everywhere and, oftentimes, we created it. *We stink.*

But that's when love steps in. God, Jesus, love "is atonement for our sins, and not only for ours, but for the whole cosmos," writes John.[48] Love doesn't condemn us for flushing the toilet. Heck, flushing the toilet is supposed to be a good thing! Love takes us up to the shower, and when we wash ourselves in even more inescapable sin, hands us a clean washcloth to scrub every square centimeter of it away. God is not a deity which love is but a part of; instead, God is love. As

---

47 Romans 7:15-20.

48 1 John 2:2.

in the love between a child and their mother. That love is God. The loving that happens when lovers are one. That loving is God. The love demonstrated in the resistance of oppression. That love is God. The love shown in the act of scrubbing our sin away. That is God.

For love cleans us all over, and over, and over again, no matter how hard we are to love.

No matter what—because restoration is what love is all about.

7

FIRE GONE COLD

We've all had those people who we just knew had our backs no matter what. Only a few months into college, I met a young man who, little to my knowledge, would become one of those people for me.

We had shared a few classes that first quarter and then both ended up staying on campus for the weeklong Thanksgiving holiday, giving us ample time to get to know each other and facilitate a fair amount of mutually manifested mischief. As the week drew on, we became quite tired of the gloomy, albeit warm, indoors and the limited escapades it provided. So, we decided to venture into the cold out-of-doors for my new friend's first-ever camping experience.

That November was an especially chilly one and, due to the adverse weather, my *classic* ruby-red 1996 Toyota Corolla, Gurdy, had decided to bother me by occasionally opting not to start. While holding my breath and crossing my fingers, I pressed the brake, pushed fully into the clutch, and turned the key. Much to our relief, the car started, and my new friend, let's call him "Tommy" (although his real name is Jordan), and I were off to our local white and wintry mountains.

Once we had driven 200 or so kilometers to the local "Alps," I parked the car and pulled out a pair of beat-up park skis which had been recently donated to me. Strapping the skis and their boot counterparts to my already-filled pack, I began trudging towards the lake with Tommy close behind. As we seemed to be following some kind of trail through the thickly wooded forest, each step felt quite firm on the compacted snow, it wasn't until after about a kilometer or two of walking amongst the trees that we finally realized we had actually been circling the very lake our young eyes had been seeking all along. (I know, we're a bit stupid.)

Minutes after this realization, Tommy and I came across a vacant yurt, sitting only ten or so meters from the lake's shore. Busting down the door—after knocking, of course—we found it to be most certainly abandoned. For a moment, we contemplated sleeping in the yurt, then decided against it since we were there to "rough it" out in the elements. It would not have been a real camping experience for my dear friend, Tommy, were we to stay inside! As an alternative, we moved thirty meters down the shoreline, where the views were nearly as spectacular, and set up our tent. After the tent was up and we had been sitting down for a while, things started to get cold. Like *cold*, cold. Tommy mentioned that a fire might be nice, and so we decided to go back to the yurt and get some of the dry firewood we had seen stowed away inside.

It was probably only seven or eight that evening when the nearly-full moon began to rise and our stargazing vista was quickly shrouded by passing clouds. We had already dug a small hole in the snow and soon placed our plundered wood in it. After some fiasco with the now wet paper towels we had brought, our fire finally lit, and we soon had quite the blaze going. We were warm. Like *warm*, warm.

Fast forward an hour or two and the evening's conversation had drifted from girls, to politics, to nature, to our plans and aspirations for the future. As we cooked and then consumed a hearty ramen noodle and oatmeal dinner, our talking slowed and we began preparing for a cold night in the tent—kept safe from the elements only by our summer sleeping bags and a couple of picnic blankets. By the time 10 p.m. rolled around, our firewood was nearly gone, laid to rest in a now much-larger fire pit.

Not long after tucking our last log into its bed of coals and tucking our conversation into the tent, we noticed several voices coming from the other side of the lake. And sure enough, far off down the shore, we saw lights bobbing up and down. Soon a small caravan was upon us. In the darkness, I could make out two full-sized humans dragging sleds behind them which housed two more fun-sized versions of the breed.

As they reached our encampment, the tallest silhouette among them spoke in a deep, friendly voice, "Hey there! How are you tonight? What a nice little fire you've got going there!"

"Thanks!" we replied cheerfully, waking our voices from their slumber, "Glad to have found some wood that wasn't frozen!"

After a few more friendly exchanges, they bid us goodnight and pushed on another thirty meters or so *to the yurt*. The very place we had purged of firewood only hours before. The small humans jumped from their sleds and ran inside, screaming with excitement. Their parents, too, sounded glad to have finally reached the comfort of the shelter. We, however, did not share in their jubilee.

Immediately, our stomachs knotted up. We had just taken, and subsequently burnt, nearly all of that kind family's firewood. The wood stove that was to keep those four from freezing was without most of its fuel. And we felt absolutely terrible.

Not much later, the two adults, and their now empty sleds, exited the shelter and made their way back towards our tent. *We're really in for it now*, I thought, *I'm probably going to go to jail for stealing firewood that I thought was just sitting there, hibernating, all winter long!* Sheepishly, we waved to them as they passed. They smiled and waved back, wishing us a good night once again. As soon as they were out of earshot, we collectively breathed a sigh of relief, knowing that jail was not on the docket for this particular camping trip, and went about readying ourselves for bed.

Soon, however, we again heard the "crunch-crunch-crunch" of their boots, and the sliding of their now-full sleds heading back towards us. We knew the inevitable was about to take place. As they passed, Tommy again waved, awkwardly, and broke the silence: "Hey, so that was your firewood in the yurt, huh?"

"Yes," the deep, kind voice replied.

Tommy continued, "Well, we took a lot of it and used it tonight …"

Cutting him off, the tall human replied, "We know, it's alright, no hard feelings. Have a good night, you guys."

Shocked by their compassion, we thanked them profusely and blew kisses in the dark as they journeyed the final stretch towards their encampment where they were greeted by shrieks of joy coming from their fun-sized human companions.

It was a very chilly night for Tommy and I once the fire went cold. But I barely recall the freezing weather. Instead, I remember falling asleep thinking about how that couple had already known we had taken the wood and yet chose not to say anything about it to us. And when we did come clean, they acted like it wasn't a big deal even though they might have had to shiver for the rest of the night, or worse, the rest of their weekend. I really couldn't understand it.

The next morning, after shivering all night, I exited the tent and quickly installed my feet into my two new ski boots. After trying to squeeze my frozen flesh into what felt like lead molds, I stood up in great discomfort and realized that our tent and firepit were sitting in the middle of a two-lane, snow-covered road that surrounded the entire lake. Embarrassed by my lack of proper camp-finding skills, I notified the sleeping Tommy and the two of us quickly went about repairing the road by filling in our gaping fire pit with snow. Dark, charcoal-infused snow, but snow nonetheless.

Once the repair was completed, we dismantled the tent and decided it was finally time for me to learn how to ski. Having never really skied before, save at a bunny hill during elementary school, Tommy came to the conclusion that it would be in my best interest to simply ski back to the car via the road we had just spent the night on.

I had watched the Olympics a time or two, so I knew that plenty of people, oftentimes folks of Norwegian descent like myself, would win gold medals by skiing cross-country. Little did I know at the time, but there is a vast difference between an old beat-up pair of park skis and a lightweight cross-country set-up. Needless to say, I certainly know the difference now.

Each "step" seemed far too difficult. I would strain to pull one ski and heavy boot far enough above the surface of the snow to allow a little wiggle motion, so as to gain some semblance of forward momentum, as I slid on the opposite ski. I would then do a little hop and switch legs so that the once grounded ski could become airborne, and vice versa. This went on for what seemed like an eternity, much to my chagrin and the great pleasure of my companion.

By the time we had reached the parking lot, the young family, with sleds in tow, had already passed us on the way back to their car. They smiled and waved, occasionally giggling amongst themselves. I have no doubt the memory of their family trip will not long be forgotten. Since the boy who had stolen their wood the night before was subsequently caught trying to downhill ski the very flat road he had camped on, before getting back to the parking lot where he couldn't even manage to get his car to start. What a fiasco!

Now to me, that family of two big people and two fun-sized people seemed a whole lot like Jesus. A whole lot like love. Hear me out on this one: I sin, I fall short of perfection constantly. Every day! (Can you believe it?) But in God's great love, God intentionally chooses not to condemn me. Instead, God makes the decision to forgive me, even when I have stolen God's proverbial firewood, the very thing that keeps God from suffering. God sleeps cold so that I can be warm. Then, when I mess up and bring park skis to a road race, God laughs and giggles alongside me. God doesn't hate me for messing up, oddly enough, God only loves me for it. Paul said that love "does not take account of the evil deed."[49] Which means that no matter how many times we mess up, God doesn't keep tabs on all of the firewood we've stolen.

So that instead of condemnation, there is grace. Because the grace we show each other is God.

This is that counterintuitive justice the Bible speaks to. And it reminds me of this famous little line in John's gospel where Jesus says that "For God so loved the cosmos as to give the Son, the only one, so that everyone having faith in him might not perish, but have the life of the Age."[50] We love this verse—I mean I mentioned it just a couple of chapters back! John 3:16 gets all of the tattoos and bumper stickers. My wife, a southern California native, even pointed out that it's printed on the bottom of In-N-Out cups! No doubt, it's a beautiful bit of prose, but we all too often forget what follows it. Because if you are someone like me who falls short of living a life of only love, the next verse is massively important. This is what Jesus, God, *love*, thinks of you: "For God sent the Son into the cosmos not that he

---

49 1 Corinthians 13:5.

50 John 3:16.

might pass judgement on the cosmos, but that the cosmos might be saved through him."[51]

This verse, if taken to heart, can be huge depending on what kind of church or what kind of family you may have been raised in. God didn't send God's son into the messy world to condemn the messy world *but to save the messy world.* Jesus wasn't sent to get in the faces of all of the messy people and tell them, "Don't you realize what a mess you are?" But instead, God came into the lives of messy people like you and me to show us a path out of our messes.

The gospels make this point so very clear. One morning Jesus is up early to go and hang out at the temple, the epicenter of the Jewish universe, where he sits down to teach and talk. While he's there, some of the religious elites bring a lady by who we're told had been caught in the act of adultery. Whether or not the claim was true, no matter if she had been set up or not, she's certainly humiliated and most likely naked. The leaders then propose a riddle to Jesus: "this woman has been caught in the very act of committing adultery; now, in the Law Moses enjoined us to stone such a person; so what do you say?"[52] Their endgame here was to try and get Jesus to say something they could use against him because they hated him —he was a threat to everything which kept them in power and kept their pockets lined. But Jesus doesn't buy in to their trivial games and instead we're told that Jesus:

> Bending down, wrote upon the ground with his finger. But, when they continued to question him, he stood up straight and said to them, "Let whosoever among you is without sin be the first to cast a stone at her." And again, bending down, he wrote on the ground. And, hearing this,

---

51 John 3:17.

52 John 8:4-5.

they departed one by one, beginning with the older of them, and he was left alone with the woman before him. And Jesus, standing up straight, said to her, "Madam, where are they? Does no one condemn you?" And she said, "No one, Lord." And Jesus said, 'Neither do I condemn you."[53]

If you grew up going to church, you've likely heard this story before. This lady has been accused of adultery. If we are to take the story literally, she's probably messed-up her marriage and maybe someone else's, too. She's destroyed what reputation she may have had because now everybody in the community knows exactly what she's done and knows exactly who she is. And after a conversation with her accusers, it says Jesus stands-up and tells her, "I do not condemn you!" In other words, "I do not sentence you to what you deserve." As shocking as this may be, we really shouldn't expect anything less from Jesus— because God did *not* send God's son into the world to condemn the world.

Let that sink in for a moment.

Jesus didn't come into the world to get in the faces of all of us sinners and call us out on our shortcomings. That's not a God of love, that's a god of guilt. And nowhere do I find, "God is guilt." Instead, God came into the lives of messed-up people to rescue us from everything that holds us back. It's a rescue plan of love. God did not send God's son into the world to condemn the world but to *save it.* Love saves the world and it chases us relentlessly. God is recorded by the ancient Hebrew author Isaiah as saying, "I was ready to be sought out by those who did not ask, to be found by those who did not seek me. I said, 'Here I am, here I am,' to a nation that did not call on my name."[54] This God takes initiative to connect with people who neither

---

53 John 8:6-11.

54 Isaiah 65:1.

asked for God, nor sought God out. Because that is exactly what love does.

God doesn't condemn.

Love acquits.

8

THE HATE WE GIVE

Okay, I get it, you may be thinking. *God, love, whatever you call it, Niq, is great. It doesn't condemn, instead it acquits. But seriously, how do we deal with the places where God doesn't look like love at all? Are you just going to brush over all of that nastiness?*

Now let me level with you—my journey towards seeing God as only love didn't begin until, while in high school, I came across a place in 1 John which says that, "God *is* love."[55] To which I was all like, *Heck yeah! I like this God. You know me, I'm all about that peace and love. That's the good stuff.* So, because of this one verse, I started reading more of the Bible, and I spent a lot of time reading about Jesus in the book of Luke, where he was always hanging out with and blessing those of lesser status, racially, economically, and socially. He said stuff like, "How blissful the destitute, for yours is the Kingdom of God," which I, for one, think sounds pretty good.[56] I liked that take on life. The more I read, the more I was like, *Yeah, this is my kind of God! This is the kind of God I would actually enjoy being in a relationship with.*

Growing up, I sometimes heard that God was kind of mean and was always watching for when I did things wrong so as to punish me. I heard that whenever bad things happened it was because God

---

55 1 John 4:8. Emphasis added.

56 Luke 6:20.

wanted them to happen. Maybe you were taught things like this, too. I remember hearing once that if I was lucky enough to make it to heaven, everyone would sit down with their popcorn and pretzels to watch all of the bad things I did during my life on a jumbotron! How terrifying! And while I had never experienced deep and intimate romantic love before, I was pretty sure that this guilt and shame I was feeling wasn't at all a part of what a loving God looked like. In fact, I was certain that love meant something else altogether. You can imagine how ecstatic I was to find, there in John's letter, how loving God might really be! That the narrative of salvation might not be so much a question of final location, such as heaven or hell, as it is a redeeming story arc revealing the heaven we all are by the gracious removal of the hell inside us by a God who is love in God's very being.[57]

But then my inherent pessimism came into frame. Maybe you can relate here. I became worried that a God of only love who invites us into only love is just too good to be true. And sometimes, passing through the Old Testament, I would totally agree with my pessimistic thoughts, especially when reading God say something like: "I will take vengeance on my adversaries, and will repay those who hate me. I will make my arrows drunk with blood, and my sword shall devour flesh."[58]

Wait, what? You may now be asking, *I thought God never changes?*[59] *God is eternal, and doesn't "eternal" mean "changeless"?*[60] And I'd have to agree with you, I've always heard that God was, is, and will be *forever.* Yet God's flesh-devouring sword seems to be in stark contrast to that

---

57 See Ilaria Ramelli, *A Larger Hope?* Vol. 1, 11.

58 Deuteronomy 32:41-42.

59 E.g. Hebrews 13:8; Malachi 3:6.

60 See Craig Keener, *IVP Bible Background Commentary: New Testament*, 665.

God of love, mercy, and grace I want to cling to from many places in the New Testament. It just doesn't sound right. This isn't the Jesus who I love reading about in the gospels. It's something else entirely:

> And when the Lord your God gives it into your hand, you shall put all its males to the sword. You may, however, take as your booty the women, the children, livestock, and everything else in the town, all its spoil. You may enjoy the spoil of your enemies, which the Lord your God has given you. Thus you shall treat all the towns that are very far from you, which are not towns of the nations here. But as for the towns of these peoples that the Lord your God is giving you as an inheritance, you must not let anything that breathes remain alive. You shall annihilate them.[61]

Okay, so just reading that I feel a little pit in my stomach. *This is God too? This is a God of love? Who loves all people? Equally? What is going on?* I honestly want to give up on God and become a full-blown atheist after reading crap like that. The theologian Greg Boyd actually counted and found thirty-seven genocidal commands, not suggestions, *commands* from God scattered throughout the Old Testament.[62] Like, if we read that area of scripture at face-value, God is some kind of a divine Pol Pot, Adolf Hitler, or Talaat Pasha. On top of those literally nation-ending orders, there are plenty of other places where humans attribute their violent acts to God, saying that God had blessed their rage, rape, and conquest. I think the prominent atheist scholar, Richard Dawkins, said it best in his book *The God Delusion*:

> The God of the Old Testament is arguably the most unpleasant character in all fiction: jealous and proud of it; petty, unjust, unforgiving control-freak; a vindictive, bloodthirsty, ethnic cleanser; a misogynistic,

---

61 Deuteronomy 20:13-17.

62 See Gregory Boyd, *Crucifixion of the Warrior God*, 294.

homophobic, racist, infanticidal, genocidal, filicidal, pestilential, megalo-maniacal, sadomasochistic, capriciously malevolent bully.[63]

I can't even say half of those words! But I think Dawkins has hit the nail on the head. Just spend fifteen or twenty minutes thumbing through many sections of the Old Testament, and God doesn't look all that loving. Or even take a look at Revelation, the finale to the New Testament, through the lens of either dispensationalist or preter-ist interpretation, and again, God doesn't look all that loving.

So how do we deal with this tension? A God of love? A God of war? Some say that God defines both of those things, therefore, they are not in contrast with one another.[64] But I mean, let's be honest, those things *are* in stark contrast with each other. Reading through these places in scripture makes me afraid that love is but a figment of my imagination. That love, in and of itself, cannot exist without violence, war, and pain to balance it out. That God is not who God says God is, and that God is something else entirely.

Needless to say, I was confused, utterly, as to the nature of God. That is, until this happened.

My lungs were about to collapse.

Each exhale concluded with the sudden urge to cough followed by my frantic inability to do so. Every four or five minutes I had to stop, head resting on a walking stick, for fear that the vertigo I had been experiencing, in conjunction with the sporadic moonlight dispersed

---

63 Richard Dawkins, *The God Delusion*, 31. Dawkins' classic book should be required reading for anyone who claims to believe in the divine.

64 An example of this perspective can be found in Francis Chan & Preston Sprinkle's book, *Erasing Hell*, 162-163.

through the trees, would have me end in some kind of muddled collapse. It was 7 p.m. I had only been awake for twelve hours, but all I wanted to do was fall over on the scree, up which I was hiking, and go to sleep.

My good friend Chad and I were hiking back to the parking lot after climbing what I thought was going to be a simple Cascade peak. However, after spending the entire summer prior to this excursion in the flatlands of Ohio, it turns out no climb is so simple.

We had made good time hiking in on Friday evening, leaving the parking lot around 5:30, and arrived at a pristine alpine lake, 1000 gained meters and eight kilometers away, no later than eight. The sun had set at least an hour before, and the ever-glorious stars of the Milky Way were visible, unaffected by the polluting lights of cities and suburbia, at a 360-degree view around the lake. I was asleep in what seemed like only moments; lying on my bedroll which rested on a soft, dry patch of grass only a meter or so away from the glassy waters of the alpine paradise. The next morning we were up by seven, and after consuming a hearty breakfast of oats and crackers, packed up our bedrolls and camp stoves to begin our ascent up the peak's long western ridge. A few hours later, we had climbed nearly a thousand meters of scree slopes and craggy shelves to the majestic white granite blocks a few hundred meters below the peak's summit pinnacle. It was breathtaking. The entire time Chad, true to his nature, had been advertising our ascent to the world around us. Be it Bigfoot, butterfly, or bear, he was attempting to speak their language and let them know how wonderful of a day we were having.

Upon arriving at the parking area the night before, we had been astonished at the amount of parked vehicles in the lot waiting for their owners to get back and warm them up. So, as one might imagine, we were surprised not to have crossed paths with any of the car's owners on such an abnormally bright and clear October weekend—somehow, we had the entire mountain all to ourselves. Talk about an ideal situation!

It was nearing twelve noon when I arrived at the first sections of actual climbing. Slowed by Chad's lack of enthusiasm for all of the scree hiking, he yelled at me from below to start up the first chimney without him and I happily complied with his request. I figured that if he got scared, I could pull the rope out of my pack, throw an end down to where he was, and then belay him up to me. He'd be safe if he so desired. To my surprise, Chad never got scared enough to use the rope. Even through a section just below the summit block advertised as having "airy steps," with a thousand or so meters of air standing between us and a nasty-looking glacier below, Chad kept his cool and pushed on.

After the traditional summit selfie and a couple of classic mountaintop pats-on-the-back, we began our descent. On the way down, instead of scenic "airy steps" and solid scrambling blocks, we were met with endless amounts of dusty scree and blocky choss. As we traversed down the opposite east ridge of the peak, we eventually descended into a massive rock-laden couloir aptly named for the equally massive Columbia River. It was there that my knees really started to feel the burn. Although, I suppose 1500 meters of downhill scree-skiing in less than two kilometers would have a certain way of doing that for just about anyone.

Once we had reached the valley floor, our sights became set on the ridge above us. It had already taken us several hours to reach the valley's bottom from the summit. Our delayed pace was in large part due to my inability to move as quickly scree-skiing as I could snow-skiing. Looking up, the thought of my having to climb another 600 meters, just to momentarily gain a ridge from which we would descend a thousand more to the car, wasn't all that appealing.

Ohio has killed me, I thought, heart thumping and lungs screaming for air, *or at least it is killing me.*

Chad, who had spent his summer away from the flatlands, didn't seem at all phased by our little uphill hike. He was ahead of me on the trail, often saying cheerful and encouraging things in empathy with my struggle. Chad had been a bit nervous earlier while soloing those airy steps below the summit block during which I was sure to make fun of his limited progress while working our way to the mountain's top. But this was different. I wasn't scared. And he wasn't making fun of me. I was exhausted. In pain. I honestly just wanted to sleep—or die. Yet, Chad kept his cheery comments coming in my direction.

Parched, hungry for Taco Bell (or really any kind of taco), with my heart rate out of control, I forced myself to stop and sit every few minutes so as to momentarily slow the torrentius "thu-thump" which echoed in my chest, neck, and wrists. The darkness, which had only recently enveloped the valley I was so desperately working to make my way out of, propagated my already frazzled state. Historically speaking, I don't usually get all that winded while climbing a mountain, let alone while walking up a little hill, but this was different. So very different! I wanted to cough, but there was no fluid anywhere inside of me to cough up.

From above me on the hill, I heard Chad's warm voice: "Wegian!" he shouted in reference to my Norwegian heritage, "Wegian, you're almost here! Only a few hundred more steps and you'll be on the ridge!"

At this point we were at least an hour removed from the valley below and I was unequivocally pissed to hear Chad's voice. I'm somewhat of a competitive guy, so I didn't want to be told *how close I was.* And I sure as heck didn't want to know that he had already made it there! Especially since, earlier in the day when Chad had slowed me down during a section of climbing, I had neglected to cheer him on and instead made fun of his moderate speed while I romped to the summit, alone.

Again I stopped, head resting on my hiking pole, and tried to catch my breath. Standing on the loose scree, my body bent forwards, I began to lucidly dream of sleep and food. Then, Chad's voice cut through the frey once again saying, "Wegian! You can do this! You're almost here!"

I just wanted Chad to shut up! Did he not understand that my lungs were about to collapse? Each exhale concluded with the immediate urge to cough followed by my helpless effort to do so. I had to stop, again, head resting on my hiking pole, afraid that the vertigo I had been experiencing would end my effort to gain the ridge in some kind of muddled collapse.

Chad is a kind person, perhaps the kindest I know. His intentions were pure. He had no desire to impede my ascent. In fact, he had wanted to do nothing more than encourage me onward. Yet this is my point—the funny thing about kindness, goodness, love, or whatever else you might want to call it—kindness has the tendency to enrage those who are lacking its heart themselves.

You see, I perceived Chad's kind gestures of support as vile and infuriating. Not because of who Chad is (a kind and sincere man) but because of what I was going through (a very difficult time, physically). This is to say that what we *see* is not always what is actually going on, because our lens shapes our reality. And more often than not, our lens, like mine that October evening, is broken.

This brings us right back into the heart of the tension regarding who God is and what God is really like. Is God really limitless love?[65] Or is God the petty, unjust, unforgiving control-freak that Dawkins suggests? Richard Rohr says, "It is not God who is violent. We are."[66] Let it sink in for a second. Rohr is suggesting that we are the problem; that we are the ones who project the violence we ourselves experience onto the divine.

Looking at the Hebrew Bible, this is actually fairly accurate because the ancient Hebrews, and those who wrote down and recorded much of what they did, were just like anybody else in the ancient Near East— they assumed that when a god confronts his or her foes, and when a god judges wrongdoing, they would resort to violence. We might go so far as to say that the Israelites believed that they were praising God when they credited violence to God, thinking of it as an offering of sorts, similar to animal sacrifices.[67] In the ancient Near East, you exalted your god by making them look the most ferocious; so if I won a battle against your nation, I would attribute it to my god, saying, even, that they commanded me to attack your nation and slaughter your people![68] It clearly makes sense that since Old Testament authors were influenced by their culture, just as you and I are influenced by ours, they would write their happenings down as they *perceived* them to take place. They "glorified" God by saying God told them to do incredibly nasty things. Twisted, I know.

---

65 John Hick provides a great examination of limitless divine love in his essay, "A Pluralist View," in *Four Views on Salvation in a Pluralistic World*, 29-59.

66 Richard Rohr, *The Universal Christ*, 146.

67 Anne Katrine de Hemmer Gudme, "Perspectives on the Care and Feeding of the Gods in the Hebrew Bible," *Scandinavian Journal of the Old Testament*: 178.

68 Greg Boyd, *Cross Vision*, 93.

But if we step back for a second, enlarging our lens, and take a look at any sliver or segment of humanity's history, we see that, by and large, the only way human justice is carried out is through violence. If someone kills my mother or father, there is a good chance that, in some regions, the perpetrator would be sentenced to death themselves for the crime. An eye for an eye. A tooth for a tooth. A life for a life. This is just how things go when we're in charge. But God, God is nothing like us. Yes, we're made in God's image, but we're broken images; cracked mirrors if you will. We reflect the divine, sure, but our reflections pale in comparison to the whole mosaic. It is the cross that shows us God is nothing like many of the Old Testament writers presumed, and that God is insurmountably bigger than the boxes we provide God with. The cross teaches us how God judges sin, not us. As in the cross represents a judgement on the sins of the world—not all sinners—it was sin that was sentenced to death on the cross.[69]

Rohr goes on to say that, "The problem of divine love is settled forever from God's side. In our insecurity, we keep re-creating 'necessary sacrifices.'"[70] We humans, since long before the Old Testament was penned, are the ones who have projected our violent nature onto the self-sacrificial, nonviolent God manifested in Jesus' life-giving death on the cross. For when Jesus bore our sin (as in he internalized the atrocious sin we committed against him in choosing to murder love itself), his death didn't purchase us back from an angry God; instead, Jesus *is* the gracious God who played by God's own rules and chose to be killed rather than kill—God chose to be murdered rather than murder. Tom Wright notes, "The gospels offer us not so much a dif-

---

69 See Revelation 20:13-14; As Bradley Jersak comments in his book, *Her Gates Will Never Be Shut*, 23: "Christ ultimately triumphs. Death and Hades must give up their dead and then come to their own decisive terminus."

70 Richard Rohr, *The Universal Christ*, 146.

ferent kind of human, but a different kind of God: a God who, having made humans in his own image, will most naturally express himself in and as that image-bearing creature; a God who ... will most naturally express himself in and as [a] pain-bearing, horror-facing creature."[71] Put simply, God takes in the horror we create so that we don't have to. And when it's all said and done, love is all that is left for us.

God is not violent. *We are.* God is not cruel. Instead, God is patient, waiting, never turning away from any of us even when we create the worst of circumstances for ourselves and, in all reality, for God, too.[72] Just because various biblical authors chose to focus on the negative aspects of their lives and attribute them to God, doesn't mean we must follow suit.[73] In fact, the metaphors and myths in scripture are true and good, not because their stories are all true or good, but precisely because in them we can see the glimmer of a good God shining through. That even in the violence attributed to God in the Hebrew Bible, we can find love if we take the time to dig.

My negative reaction to Chad's encouragement that October evening was unnecessary. I recall attempting to shout a few unsavory words in his direction as I made my way up the hill that fateful night. For some reason, I hated Chad for his kindness even though he was actually there to cheer me along the entire way.

Friends, love is self-sacrificial. In the upside-down kingdom of God, mightiness is expressed not through slaying one's enemy but instead by subjecting oneself to be slain. Even when we wish the worst upon

---

71 N.T. Wright, *How God Became King*, 104.

72 Alden Thompson makes a great case for God's never-wavering patience in the sixth chapter of his book, *Who's Afraid of the Old Testament God?*, 99-123.

73 This point is nicely articulated by Matthew Korpman during an examination of Hell as presented in the gospels in his book, *Saying No to God*, 264-265.

God, God wishes the best upon us. Even when we kill God, God redeems us. This is what it looks like to be mighty.[74] For love does not care that it gets taken advantage of. In fact, love walks into a situation knowing it will give and yet receive nothing in return. Love is only love *because that is its very nature.* The very love we see all around us, all of the time, is God. And through the narrative of the cross, where God dies so that God's creation would not have to, we see most clearly the passion of the divine: self-sacrificial, horror-facing love.

A love far more infinite than any human hostility towards it.[75]

---

74 See Isaiah 9:6.

75 Paraphrased from Robin Parry & Ilaria Ramelli, *A Larger Hope?* Vol. 2, 208.

9

COMING IN CLUTCH

So, God is nonviolent … great, you may be thinking, *I like the sound of that, but that's got to change, right? In the end God changes. Love must have its limits?* I used to think along the same lines, but then I spent a few summers at camp and started seeing things a little bit differently. Because I *love* summer camp. In my experience, there is no place on earth quite as cool. The staff are awesome. The campers are awesome. The activities are awesome. Days off are awesome. Heck, even the occasional sunburn is awesome if it turns into a tan!

As a kid, I had always wanted to attend a summer camp nestled on the side of a beautiful lake in northern Idaho. Advertisements were seemingly everywhere at my church: in the bulletin, on the wall-to-wall cork boards, in the greeter's hands (it was a bit excessive). Money being tight, I never actually went. That is, until the summer I was seventeen—the minimum age required to work at camp—when I could not have been any happier to be hired as a maintenance worker.

I had a blast. I fixed tons of summer camp stuff. I swam with my pals every lunch break. Ate lots of watermelon. And even got to act in a play! Life was great! So great, in fact, that I went back the next summer. I swam some more. Ate lots more watermelon. But failed to get cast in another play, which was a serious bummer.

Because of the casting director's disastrous decision, when it came time to apply for the following summer, I decided that I wanted to take my acting prowess to another camp. A camp that would appreciate my talents for what they were—*genius*. Low and behold, after auditions, I was cast in five plays. That's right—*five*—I'm not exaggerating. I was to be a recurring character who loosely connected tails from a magical medieval land to the modern elementary classroom. It was horrendous. I was horrendous. And to make matters worse, my life wasn't all that straightened-out at the moment due to some previous incidents.

You see, only a month before, I had finally garnered up the nerve to ask a girl out for the first time. We had worked together for nearly an entire school year at our university's student association. I really liked her but was worried my feelings wouldn't be reciprocated. So, I did the only sensible thing that could keep our friendship alive while testing out the possibility of a romantic future together: I asked her to join me on a homework assignment. As my friend, Paddy, later said, "In typical Niq fashion, he was killing two birds with one stone." In my mind, of course, this was a date. In hers, it probably sounded like a lot of hard work for nothing much at all. I mean, I wasn't even buying her dinner!

I was taking a humanities course in music appreciation, as all good first-year undergraduates do, and needed to visit the local opera so as to fulfill a course requirement. I popped the question one day at work as we were setting up canopies on the lawn in front of the engineering building, "Hey, so, uh, well, um, hey, Jo" (which was, and still is, her name). "So, ehh, well, do you, um, maybe, err, want to help me, um, with my, my homework Thursday night?"

"What time?" she said eloquently.

"Uh, well, um, hey, so ehh, yeah about that, yeah, during work Thursday night at the, uh, opera."

I know, this dialogue is only three sentences in and you're probably already confused. Let me translate it for you: I wanted to grow old with this Jo person, so I asked her to play hooky from work and to come to the opera with me. She agreed. I was ecstatic.

I took my ruby-red 1996 Toyota Corolla, Gurdy, and cleaned her both inside and out. I scrubbed and vacuumed. Polished and scraped. Gurdy was looking good! And I was more than ready for the homework assignment!

Jo and I actually had a pretty good time skipping out on work that fateful Thursday night. Maybe it was the clean car, or maybe it was the fact that we were the only ones dressed-up at the opera that particular evening. Or it could have been because Jo pretended to know a lot about music even though she didn't. But low and behold, not more than a week after that initial "romantic" encounter, we exchanged the fabled "I like you" phrase. And only a week after that, exchanged the even more fabled "I love you," followed by our first kiss. You might be thinking, *Okay Niq, wow, slow down. This is your first relationship! Did you forget what brakes are for?* First, I want to thank you for your concerns, they mean a lot. But I had to move fast for a reason. We didn't have much time. Jo was about to take a year and go work in Belize where her mother was born and several of her extended family members still lived. And I was about to head to that new camp, with all my acting prowess in tow.

So, after saying our goodbyes at the airport and crying my little eyes out as I tried to merge into traffic, I turned Gurdy south and headed to my newest summer adventure situated on a great big lake.

It was late evening when I got out of town and onto the highway. I knew I could make good time getting to camp if I were to keep on driving into the wee hours of the morning. I stopped at a local grocer and purchased enough potassium to keep my late-night marathon alive. I peeled back the peel of my first banana and started to cry again. (Cut me some slack, guys! I wasn't going to see her for a year!) When I had stopped crying, it dawned on me that I was making pretty good time. And, about two hours in, I calculated that I might even make it to camp before midnight. I was so excited!

I rounded another corner on a beautiful Oregon highway paralleled by towering evergreens on either side. As I did, I noticed that my gas pedal, one which usually allowed my beloved car to accelerate, wasn't behaving as it should. In fact, it wasn't working at all.

I turned my wheel to the right to make my way onto the shoulder. Several times I tried to restart the car, but to no avail. I even looked under the hood and tried to Google my way out of it, but those tall pines seemed to be jamming my data signal. Nothing was behaving. So, I called my dad—the car's previous owner—and he told me to call a tow truck.

Six hours and 300 dollars later, I finally made it to camp with my car and all of its precious contents in tow. It was around four in the morning when the now-quite-wealthy tow truck driver neatly backed my car into a dirt parking space outlined by barkless logs on either side. I thanked my new friend, who the entire drive couldn't talk enough about how much he loved when it snowed in June while, coincidentally, it was snowing in June, and sent him off. As he drove away, I pulled my tent out from a storage bin in Gurdy's backseat and made quick work of assembling it in another vacant, snow-covered parking space.

Only a week after experiencing what I later learned was the blowing of my clutch, I was involved in a softball accident which tore the MCL in my right knee enough to permit me to drive those fun electric carts in grocery stores. However, without a working car, getting to any grocery store was a challenge in and of itself. Even worse, getting to doctor appointments proved to be much harder, especially if my appointment didn't coincide with my or a friend's day off.

A number of times I hitchhiked eighty kilometers to the hospital for my regular knee checkup or physical therapy appointment. I met plenty of interesting characters along the way, to be sure, and all of them were quite sympathetic to my cause since I did sport a shiny new set of crutches.

One time in particular, near the end of the summer, I had made it about half-way from the hospital back to camp before my ride had reached his destination. I was actually pretty happy to be let out. His car smelled of weed and the steering wheel was on the passenger side like he was in Britain or something. (Or maybe the fumes were getting to me? Was I tripping?) As soon as he dropped me off, I began walking, or should I say, "crutching," through town, hoping to get to the main intersection on the other side where I thought it would be easier to catch a ride headed up towards the camp.

About a kilometer or so into my "crutch," a short, middle-aged lady rolled down her passenger window and yelled in my direction, "Hey! You there! Where are you going? Yes, you!" Startled by her abrupt tone, I looked her way and floundered to find the words which described my desired destination. Not wanting to waste any time, she commanded me to get in the car. Not seeing her offer me any questionable candy, I complied without a word.

As my two silver companions and I got settled in the passenger seat, she steered the car into the road and began to scream questions in my direction. She asked about where I wanted to go, what I was doing there, and what I wanted to do with my life. I know, she hit hard with those big philosophical life questions, and we were only a few minutes into the drive! Had I not been nearly two meters tall and nineteen years old I might have thought this lady wanted to kidnap me! However, as we drove along, I realized the woman who sported the incredibly loud voice box was a deeply kind individual. In fact, I later learned that she had actually driven over sixty kilometers out of her way to drop me off less than a hundred meters from my bunk. Talk about breathtaking kindness.

As kind as many of my rides may have been, that summer was very frustrating for me. Not only because I sustained the knee injury during my first (and only) at-bat of the season, but also because my nineteen-year-old idea of freedom had all but been taken away. I may have only had one leg, but I had no working wheels whatsoever! I was bummed to say the least.

I wanted to climb mountains and big rock walls with my friends, yet because of my knee injury, that was not a possibility. So much as getting to a trailhead was in and of itself hopeless. There I was, busted leg, busted car, new long-distance relationship, bad acting skills, with only a week left before I would be out of work and permanently stranded eighty kilometers from the nearest hospital. I put out a desperate all points bulletin to my fellow staff members—if anyone who knew more about cars than me would be so kind as to install a brand new, generically branded clutch which I had procured from the internet, they would be handsomely rewarded with my thanks. And that's when a gentleman we'll call, Hephaestus, answered my plea.

Hephaestus sacrificed much of his free time during that final week of camp, well over forty hours worth, to repair my clutch. First, we jacked-up the front of the car—still sitting in the same dirt parking spot which it had been left in by my late-night, snow-loving tow truck pal three months before—then, after I placed some cardboard on the ground to reduce our chances of getting dirty, we got to work. By the end of our first hour under the hood, I realized that knowing how to change the oil was really only scratching the surface regarding car innards. I was covered from head to toe in grease and various other fluids after unscrewing just a bolt or two! I have never enjoyed a shower more than after those days spent under Gurdy.

Occasionally, while completing various tasks around camp, I would pass by the car and find Hephaestus under the hood, feverishly working to replace my clutch. He said that he enjoyed replacing clutches and that this was to be his third replacement in as many years. I couldn't imagine anyone enjoying fixing something so broken, or loving a task so dirty. But for some reason, he did. And Hephaestus was willing to give up much to make not just my week, but my life, a whole lot better.

If you've ever seen a picture or painting intended to represent Jesus' death, you've probably noticed the other two fellas hanging on crosses to his left and right. While up there, Jesus has a conversation with them, men who had to have messed-up pretty bad in life, bad enough to have been sentenced to death by Roman crucifixion:

> And one of the criminals hanging there insulted him: "Are you not the Anointed? Save yourself and us." But the other, rebuking him, said, "Do you not fear God, since you are under the same sentence? And we have received a return of the things due for the things we did; but this man did nothing wrong." And he said, "Jesus remember me when you come into your Kingdom." And he said to him, "Amen, I tell you, today you will be with me in paradise."[76]

Jesus says to this mess of a man, "You are already in paradise; right here, right now." This is a criminal! A guy who sucked at life, even by human standards! A guy who messed up! And yet Jesus is saying,

---

76 Luke 23:39-43.

"Don't sweat it, pal! I've got you, Love has you now. We run our show by a different metric, one that isn't based on how messy you are, but by how clean love is."

Having a mess or being a mess isn't anything new. We've all made unwise choices that sent us way beyond what we see as being the point of no return. But no matter who you are, I want you to know this, to hear this, to let what I'm about to say soak into your very soul: Regardless of your mess, God offers a solution to our sinful human condition. It's a solution that's always been inside of you, and everyone else you've ever met, even in your darkest hour. And that solution is not more money, not fame, and it's not a better job or a nice vacation either.

The solution is something far more transcendent. It's the love that God was, is, and will always be—embedded deep within you.

That sounds so simple. So trendy. So naive, even. I know. But love, the personality of the divine lodged inside of us all, really is the solution to *everything*. In a very real way that's the whole reason Jesus came. Jesus who is God. God who is only love. Only love which is our law, our duty, as pieces of Christ's body, as facets of humanity. Jesus came to show us that only love is *it*.

It's everything. It's universal. Only love is the endgame of *everyone*.

Perhaps the argument which has divided Christians for centuries is too rigid. That the Reformed tradition, which espouses that God predestines some for goodness and damns others to destruction, is compatible with Arminianism where free will is at play. That for a god to truly be of love, that God would have to be rooted in free will yet have a bias towards our predestined good, our predestined adoption. So that in the end there really will be only love. I hope this with confidence because I know firsthand that love doesn't pull back from messy people. Instead, it loves the mess. Transformation, process, and evolution are the goal. Perfection is but a waste of time. Because as we progress towards love, love becomes all.[77]

Love is both our liberator from bondage and the reality of our futures.[78] Love loves fixing broken things, messy things. It loves getting dirty alongside us, under the hood, covered in oil and grease. Always by our side, leading, guiding, and teaching. When we feel stuck, it is there to drive us sixty kilometers out of the way to get us to a safe place. Love shows up when we need it most. When we are in the thick of it, when life sucks, love runs towards the mess and says, "You're coming with me."

Love is always there and it will always be there. Love doesn't go away; Jesus was just getting the party started. Paul says that love "tolerates all things, has faith in all things, hopes in all things, endures all things."[79] Meaning it will wait *past* the end, because love will last forever.[80]

It has no limits. Love is infinite. It cannot be earned and it cannot be done away with because love is simply what *is*.[81]

For love is God.

---

77 Titus 2:11; 2 Peter 3:9; 1 Corinthians 15:22.

78 See James Sire, *The Universe Next Door*, 286.

79 1 Corinthians 13:7.

80 See 1 Corinthians 13:8.

81 Julie Ferwerda makes this point in her book, *Raising Hell*, 80.

10

THE FINGER PUPPET

One of my favorite artists, David Hayward, drew a cartoon where people are penciling boxes around themselves on an infinite plain—boxes and boundaries as far as the eye can see. And yet, standing amidst the divisions, there is Jesus, holding a pencil upside down, erasing the lines of division which were entirely made-up to begin with.[82]

The first time I saw the cartoon my stomach churned. Growing up in an individualistic culture means I was taught to think in terms of us-versus-them—maybe you were, too: a "dualistic mind" some call it. It is taught in sports where there is only one Stanley Cup champion, in popular culture where there is only one Oscar for best picture, in church where there is only one select group of the redeemed, and so on. But no matter your anthropological persuasion, you can't argue that our human divisions are *human* made: religion, nationality, culture, language, and politics are all things we brought into existence and things we chose to let divide us. Then, we go about bickering amongst ourselves, claiming that the proverbial square we are in is best, and those who are with us in it are right. Meaning that, sadly, the things which we allow to divide us are the things *we* created. So, how do we begin to advocate for the radical erasing ways of Jesus? To

---

82 You can see David's cartoon for yourself (and purchase a print if you'd like) on his website at www.nakedpastorstore.com/products/eraser.

try my hand at answering it, let me tell you another story—a story about the summer my life changed forever.

I remember sitting in my parent's silver Ford Escape parked in our garage, wanting to sleep in the car so that I would be more than ready to go in the morning. It was a Saturday night in mid-August, and the next morning I was going to *real* school for the very first time. Being homeschooled for a decade had made me quite the socially deprived youngling and so, had you been in my shoes, I bet you would have been excited, too. That Sunday morning we awoke quite early and drove the three hours to a small boarding academy nestled in the wheat fields of eastern Washington where I was to begin classes the next day. As excited as I may have been, I still had one problem: boarding schools cost money. I had sent out letters asking for people to sponsor me. I took summer jobs working both as a ranch hand as well as a research assistant at our county museum (the two closest things I could think of to becoming a real-life Indiana Jones). I worked my tail off as a "chef" in the cafeteria once I got to campus to make the experience somewhat affordable.

On our way to the campus that morning, we passed through a town cleverly named "George" and arrived just before the start of registration.[83] I was ecstatic. *Finally,* I thought, *I'm going to have friends outside of my homeschool choir!* And, boy oh boy, did registration day exceed my expectations. I moved into my dorm room, got my hours scheduled for working in the cafeteria, took a tour of the campus, and received my first ever computer from the IT department. Later

---

83 George, Washington—get it?

on, they had burgers for dinner and a handshake line where everyone, all of the staff, teachers, and students, greeted each other and traded names. I'd never been so happy to exchange germs with three hundred people in such a short period of time! Despite the excitement of the day, I had trouble sleeping that night as my nerves about what real classes and real teachers would be like began to get the best of me.

The next morning I awoke, barely able to breathe from the butterflies rumbling about inside my stomach. My first class was scheduled for 7:15 a.m., and I arrived at the building well over an hour early while it was still pitch black outside. I was surprised that the building was unlocked at such an hour. I sat in the darkened hall in silence with only my pounding heart to keep me company.

My fellow classmates began to arrive only a few minutes before the first bell which signaled three minutes until class. Once our teacher unlocked the classroom door, we all filed in, and I sat down in my first ever school desk. The desk was black with paint chipping up and down all of its legs. The wooden desktop was obviously well-used, sporting both graphite graffiti and peeling stickers, but I paid no mind. I was overjoyed just to be going to school, no matter the quality of the desks! Overjoyed, that is, until our teacher called our attention to the front and class actually started. It was algebra class and, after cheating my way through pre-algebra in eighth grade, I was beginning to feel a bit uncomfortable about my new situation. The year before I had told my mother that I would do all of the odd problems in each day's pre-algebra chapter, all of which had answers conveniently placed in the back of the book. This proved to be an unsavory strategy in the long run as I struggled the first quarter to maintain even a low B; a grade only so high because of the generous tutoring of one of my classmates.

Math wasn't my only problem after moving away from home. Throughout all four years of high school, I always seemed to have trouble with roommates. Truth be told, my greatest fear in moving in together was that my partner, Jo, would want to move out, just as so many of my past roommates had! (So far she's stuck around. Fingers crossed.) The first roommate I had lasted into November of my freshman year; then after living by myself for a while, I moved in with a second who barely lasted three weeks. The next year my roommate and I actually made it all the way through, but it's not like we were the best of friends. During my third year, I lived with a fella who I got along with fine, that is, until he walked in on me doing what teenagers often do when they're alone. I was introduced to pornography only a few weeks into my boarding school experience and it didn't take long for it to all but envelop my life. With access to a computer, I became obsessed. And, as many folks raised in conservative Christendom do, I felt absolutely terrible about it. My upbringing had limited my exposure to the potential consequences of pornography, and when my father did have *the talk* with me, it was a bit too late to make much of a difference.

While I may have felt plagued by this and other hidden behaviors, I tried to keep my exterior persona pure. Because if I could control what people saw me do, I could, in theory, control what people *thought* about me, and I wanted people to think I was cool. So, I played on the football team. I sang in the choir. Eventually, I was hired as a resident assistant. And once I made it through algebra, I actually kept up pretty good grades! I wanted to be perfect so badly that I never missed a class, nor did I allow myself to be late since my very first day of high school. Other than receiving fifty dollars in cash at the end of each year of perfect attendance, I gained nothing from this narcissistic publicity stunt. I couldn't make starter on the football team. I couldn't make the most elite choir. I didn't get a 4.0. So instead, I tried to stake my own claim to fame—"That Niq guy doesn't miss class!" I know what you're thinking, *Oh yeah, Niq. All the cool kids do just that.*

As time went on, I realized that what the cool kids actually do is this thing called "socializing." This particular skill was not one easily learned at homeschool and so as time went on, I forcibly became more and more extroverted. So much so that conversation eventually began to flow more naturally, people seemed more engaged in what I had to say, and sometimes they even laughed at my jokes! On top of that, peers stopped making fun of me for my homeschool history, at least to my face. Life was going great. I even had the courage to *like* a girl here and there. I know, scandalous, right? (Thanks, purity culture.) That being said, I never rationalized expressing my inkling affections towards any female, save perhaps asking them to our school's dumbed-down prom, coined "banquet," for fear that it would ruin the friendship. Of course, in hindsight, I'm quite happy with that apprehension, since the first gal I dated ended up sticking around for the long-haul. Who knows what kind of relationship I would be in if I paired-up with the first girl I ever had any feelings for? That's a scary thing to think about; let's not go there.

Every quarter, my high school would dedicate an entire day of class to community service. It was a pretty cool tradition. Groups would rake leaves for the elderly, sort clothes at a second-hand store, bake sweets for the local homeless population, and so on. On my final service day in the spring of my senior year, I signed-up for a project at a center for mentally-disabled individuals. Maybe I signed-up with a girl I was crushing on? I don't remember if that part is true or not, but, for the sake of the story, let's say we even sat next to each other on the bus ride there! So obviously, if that were true, the day was going great. Upon arriving at the center, I got off of the bus with nearly a dozen other students and filed into a briefing room at the side of the building. It was dingy and small, filled with a handful of chairs and two tables. Several of us sat at the tables, while others leaned up against the back wall waiting for instructions. The center's director came in and, with the door shut behind her, briefed us on what we would be doing that day. We watched an introductory video before being shown out into the main foyer to mingle.

I found my way to the crafts table and got caught up in conversation with a local who seemed to have somewhat of a monopoly on the finger puppets. In all honesty, I have no idea what we talked about that day. But I do remember being captivated by our conversation, and crafting, for hours. By the time our group of students were all ready to leave, I had made several finger puppets all with various looks. One sported some neat brown hair and a wide, sharp face like our principal. Another had frizzy white hair, thin reading glasses, and a carefully cut long red tie like my literature teacher. Along with one which didn't exactly resemble my religion teacher, but was intended to.

As we loaded the bus, I handed the first finger puppet to the bus driver, who just so happened to be the school principal. He thought of it as a kind gesture and thanked me. That evening I tossed the horrid religion teacher creature straight into the wastebasket and began waiting anxiously for the next day's late-morning literature class where I would present my final finger puppet—my masterpiece. The classroom consisted of many of my close friends and, let me be the first to tell you, we were a rowdy bunch. Jokes and poignant sarcasm were commonplace. I'm not sure how much our English-born instructor, Mr. L, appreciated the energetic atmosphere, but he did chime in here and there with quick and cutting wit, which only encouraged our antics.

I might not always have been the loudest in the room, but I did release plenty of wise-cracks to stoke the fire from time to time. This day in particular, I was waiting for the perfect moment to present our teacher with the finger puppet I had prepared for him. About half-way through the period, my long-awaited moment had come. I stood up from my seat, three rows from the front, and pranced gingerly toward Mr. L's desk. As I handed him his doppelganger in finger puppet form, we locked eyes, just like in the movies, and I said something to the extent of, "Yesterday, we were out for our service project at the retarded people's home and I thought of you."

Utter silence. You could have heard a chia seed drop on the carpeted floor.

Our eyes were still locked, and I could feel about thirty other sets staring through the back of my head. Mr. L's face had changed posture. It's color had become bright red. Mine quickly followed suit as I realized what a hurtful thing I had just said.

"Out!" he said sternly, "Get your things and get out of my classroom! Now!"

I was devastated. Tears began rolling down my cheeks before I could even get to the door. Remember, I had never missed a class in my entire educational career. Not even a part of one. This was uncharted territory for me.

I sat in the hall outside of the classroom's wide wooden door, head between my knees, and wept. Passing students, and even a history teacher, offered their sympathies, but all had great trouble prying any information out of my choked-up self. There I was, eighteen years old, a senior in high school, crying my eyes out because I had been kicked out of class for an unbecoming presentation of a finger puppet. Not only did I conclude that I had lost what little respect I may have had from a teacher I truly admired, but I also realized how deeply I must have hurt him. In all honesty, I've never felt so terrible in all my life.

As soon as class was out, and thirty very solemn classmates had filed past, I went back inside to apologize. My tears had since dried-up and I had had plenty of time to rehearse my speech. Yet, as soon as I saw his face, my twin waterfalls renewed their lease on mine and I could barely speak. But Mr. L was gracious, more gracious than I deserved. I tearfully explained to him that what I meant to say was not that I had been at the center and the people there reminded me of him, but instead that I considered him to be a great teacher and thought of him while crafting the day before.

Needless to say, I didn't crack any jokes, in *any class*, for the rest of the quarter.

When it came time for graduation, I received a beautiful attendance award handcrafted by my woodshop teacher. The local newspaper even came out and did a story on me! I sure thought that was cool. But none of that would have happened if it were not for the unearned, undeserved kindness of Mr. L.

I hurt him beyond belief, publically no less. He had every right to mark me absent for the day. He might have been able to fail me had he been so inclined. But he didn't. That is akin to the amazing grace Philip Yancey writes of when he says, "nothing we can do that will make God love us more ... nothing we can do that will make God love us less."[84] This understanding is beyond the laws which govern this world. It's a love called "God" coming down as a human, a new Adam, to fulfill the broken covenant we were meant to keep.

As Paul pointed out, "For just as in Adam all die, so also in the Anointed all will be given life."[85] He's honing in on what Jesus was meant to do: become us all so as to rescue us all. Friends, our bro-

---

84 Philip Yancey, *What's So Amazing About Grace?*, 70.

85 1 Corinthians 15:22.

ken situation does not define us! Love, the sole, sacred, singular characteristic of the divine, intentionally chose to come into solidarity with us, its body, so that its body, all of humanity, might live. Tom Wright says that in the end "God ... will be 'all in all'; and for Paul it is the body, not just the soul, the mind or the spirit, which is the temple of the living God. The body is meant for the Lord, he says, and the Lord for the body."[86] All of you is meant for God. *All of you is meant for love.* The hidden parts. The shameful parts. The ugly parts. The guilty parts. The evil parts. God chooses for all people to be with God in a new covenant where love is the only law. Where you don't get in by following the rules, but instead by the boundless love of Love.

Because what would it mean if, as understood in so many religious sects, following the rules gained you salvation? And what would it mean for those not privileged enough to know what the rules are and how to follow them? Let's just say, for the sake of analogy, that western Christianity's conceptualization of how salvation works is 100 percent correct.[87] So, if you've done the right things, from the perspective of western Chrsitianity, you'll have a great shot at getting your ticket punched on the one-way train to heaven.

But what if you're some native chap living deep in the Amazon jungle? You've never heard of Jesus, nor will you ever. Neither have you made contact with an adherent to western Christianity who might be able to "save" you through conversion. The only thing abnormal to your context that might in some way be tied to western thought was a jetliner you once saw flying high above, which you perhaps saw as a sign of good fortune from one of your gods. Is grace not big enough

86 N.T. Wright, "Mind, Spirit, Soul and Body," *NTWrightPage*.

87 I in no way endorse the idea that western Christianity is 100 percent right, in fact, if we're to take seriously the infinite nature of the divine, I would suppose that it's far more wrong than its adherents classically assume.

for you, our Amazonian friend, in this scenario? And if it is, because of your extenuating circumstances, is it then not big enough for say a Muslim who has been exposed to the ideals of western Christianity yet, due to their upbringing and cultural heritage, thought the teachings to be heretical? Or what about the atheist who rightfully rejects a god of violence who is said to kill anyone who disobeys so much as the most trivial of command? We humans have narrowed the gates to salvation, but it seems to me that God is constantly trying to show us how infinitely wide the gates truly are—as wide as grace is deep.

Whereas all are bound in the deservance of death for being a part of the family of Adam, a family who would rather draw lines than erase them, *all* are made alive in Christ. Every single human being, whether they seek the Hebrews' YHWH, the Hindus' Brahman, or some new age transcendence, all of those impulses are a legitimate attempt at defining the one infinite God who is love itself. We are all imperfectly striving for the same thing. A thing we inherently know resides within humanity, yet exists elusively—*only love.*

It's interesting to note that the person of Jesus *never* irreversibly condemned anyone. Yes, he called loose-lipped idiots like me out on their hypocrisy, proverbially kicking them out of class, but he never flunked or failed them for their shortcomings. Instead, he forgave, erasing the imaginary boundaries we surround ourselves with. Oh were we to always see this as God's rule. Where love is the great ethical code.

The doppelganger finger puppet I made Mr. L was graciously displayed on his usually barren desk until the day I graduated and, as some have reported, long afterwards.

That's exactly what God looks like—and such love is exactly how we can begin to flip our proverbial pencils upside down too.

Because forgiveness is for all, no matter what.

11

THE GREAT KID-STOPPER BLACKOUT

Lots of people think the word "love" is a bit overused. But I kind of disagree; I need to say "I love you" more often. My partner, Jo, who by now you've heard several mentions of, reminds me of that fact more often than I'd like to admit. Jo's always been the girlfriend I've referenced because, well, she's the only girlfriend I've ever had. We met at work, started dating after several months, and then got hitched a few years later. Pretty simple story, right? Well, no, not really. As with anything else in life, our relationship has had some significant nuance.

One particularly interesting element of our relationship is the amount of time early on we spent doing long-distance. Actually, on our wedding day, we had spent 52 percent of our time in the relationship physically apart, living in different states and even, at times, different countries. Because of all the separation, I had ample opportunity to cook-up exciting engagement scenarios, my favorite of which involved a kidnapping.

The plan was to buy my best buds some ski masks. Then, I was going to have a couple of them kidnap Jo, tossing her, eyes blindfolded and limbs bound, into a rented U-Haul van. After that, they would drive her to a local airport where my pilot pal, Chad, was going to load her into the back of a little Cessna and fly her in circles for thirty minutes or so—I wanted her disoriented. Upon landing (at the same airport), they would unload her onto a grassy field where I, dressed in a suit and tie, would be waiting, on one knee, with flowers and a ring.

Romantic, right?

Well, literally everyone I told about the idea figured it would be a good way to end up in prison. Even my boss said the scenario gave him nightmares. All of my closest confidants, both friends and family, vehemently rejected what I thought was a killer proposal. So, I opted instead for an easier method—I popped the question at the top of a mountain.

Alright, so I know that sounds way colder and somehow even more hectic than a nice little kidnapping, but there were actually loads of benefits to this method. First, Jo had to hear my proposal out as she would need the rope, to which we were both attached, to get down. Not to mention that the cold forced her to hug me just to keep warm no matter what her answer might have been. Heck, the proposal was even a pretty punny idea, since it really would be a *mountaintop experience*.

I ended up going the punny route and she said, "Yes!" Well, maybe without the exclamation point. It was far too cold to say much of anything with emphasis.

We were going to get hitched. Super fun. Super cold. Super exciting. After getting off the mountain, we did all the classic arguing about how much we were going to spend on the wedding, where it was going to be, and who was going to get to roast us during the ceremony (thanks, Paddy). And after all of the important items were checked off of the list, Jo decided that she should get some kind of a kid-stopper. You know, *to stop kids from happening*.

She found a local clinic to get her kid-stopper installed and begged me to drive her there. I was reluctant and told her that I wasn't all that into medical facilities—which is still true—I avoid them like the plague. Yet Jo persisted, saying she desperately wanted me to come along for "moral support." Something about hand-holding and designated driving. So, I went. I mean I'll be honest here, it's hard to say "no" to someone you love.

By the time we pulled up to the front of our local planned parenthood clinic, my stomach was already churning. Ever since observing my mother's late-night medical emergencies as a child, I've had a very stiff aversion to anything even remotely medical. I drive by a hospital and nearly need an ambulance myself. I can't watch movies or TV shows with hospital scenes. Heck, I can't even talk to people about medical stuff without getting a little woozy! Come to think of it, I'm going to go lie down for a minute.

I'm back! I was gone for like an hour, no joke.[88]

So, where were we? Right, the two of us pulled into the clinic's parking lot and went inside. I sat down in the waiting room, and Jo went up to the reception desk to let them know she had arrived. The room was small, some old toys off in the corner, a broken TV hanging on the far wall, and a coffee table surrounded by fifteen or so chairs. The table housed a variety of magazines and I, without hesitation, went for the nearest *National Geographic*.

I was thoroughly caught up in an editorial on biomedicines when Jo's name was called. She grabbed my hand in an attempt to pull me with her, but I resisted. She gave me *the look* as she stood up, and I resisted all the more. By the time she was at the door which leads to

---

88 I wrote this chapter on April first, but I'm not kidding—I'm serious! I had to go lay down to let the lightheadedness wear off. I have a rather serious problem.

God knows what kind of modern torture machines, I was able to muster a faint wave and mutter an, "I love you" in her direction. She glared at me for what seemed like an eternity and then turned her head with a flippant flip and walked through the door frame into the sinuous hallway.

Thirty minutes and now well into a *Time* magazine later, I became a little concerned. The kid-stopping procedure Jo was supposed to be getting was only scheduled to take fifteen minutes or so, not a half-hour. I waited a while longer before finally receiving a text from her which read: "The doctor convinced me to go with an arm implant … "

That was all I needed to read.

The word "implant" immediately had my heart racing and my head spinning. Soon the whole room was going in circles and I couldn't help but think that I might want to lie down. I took a few deep breaths, closed my eyes, and did the best I could to clear my head. When I opened them the spinning had stopped. The room was still. My heart was steady. All was well.

I looked back down at the magazine and continued reading.

I don't remember much after that, except feeling like I was both in a deep sleep and about to wake up simultaneously. Not that I know what that's like or anything, because, well, I'm not really ever conscious until I'm awake. But that's what it felt like all the same. The more awake I became, the more aware I became of a relieving, warm sensation resonating from my groin. It felt watery. Nice, actually. And peaceful. I wanted to feel it more, so I released a bit more of my body's tension and more of the wonderfully warm, watery sensation came to pass. It was delightful! That is until I opened my eyes.

The first thing I saw was my shorts. They seemed to be right up next to my face. The room was upside down and my head was actually on the carpeted floor between my two knees which were also on the floor. Puzzled, I lifted my head to an upright position, only to realize that I was doing a Cold War duck-and-cover between the row of chairs and the magazine-wielding coffee table. And then I finally saw it.

The puddle.

On the floor.

Between my legs.

I tried to stand up from the strange fetal position I had found myself in but could only come-to enough to sit with my back against the chair that I, and my *Time* magazine, had once called home. Once upright, I began hearing voices, several of them all asking if I was alright. I had been alone in the lobby when the incident took place; however, that was no longer the case. Three of the clinic's four staff had gathered around, all coming to my rescue. They asked what had happened, and I responded with a simple, "Well, I think I pissed myself."

Indeed, that is exactly what I had done. I had pissed myself. I had pissed myself in the clinic's waiting room. I had pissed myself several doors away from any torturous medical supplies. I had pissed myself for no real reason at all.

A juice box and some Cheez-It crackers were in my hands within moments. I was told that I needed to consume them pronto to get me feeling back to normal. Jo came out into the waiting area only a few minutes after my episode. Prior to leaving the examination room, Jo's doctor had nonchalantly told her that, "He might have had a little accident out there." I guess she thought the whole clinic was pulling a joke on her because when Jo did come out into the lobby, she was pretty shocked that he really did "have a little accident."

All four of the clinic's staff waved to us as we walked out, Jo holding me by the arm to be sure I didn't collapse again. As we got to our car, the doctor said, smiling, "You might want to drive him home, he could use a nap!" So much for my being the designated driver.

I wish I could tell you that my experience in the planning your parenthood clinic was the last of its kind. But alas, I can't. Three months later I was in a dentist's chair and nearly the same thing happened. Thankfully, I realized what was about to occur just moments before it did, so I clenched my genitals to limit the leakage. The good news? It actually kind of worked. But, just to be safe, the next time I went to the dentist I wore an adult diaper.

For some reason, I'm just wired this way. My queasiness is inevitable in medical environments. Sometimes I've got to sit down after just thinking about getting a shot. Each of the two times I got my Covid-19 jabs, I had to mentally prepare myself for about two hours prior—meditating a while to get in sync with my chi. Other times, however, I'm not afforded the luxury of centering myself, the "water" falls, and I'm extremely embarrassed. The environment may change, but for me, the results are almost always inevitable.

The same is true of love. Love will win. Love does win. Love has won. Love is *inevitable*.

What does inevitable love look like practically? Well, Paul, in a letter he wrote to some folks in the ancient city of Corinth, said this of love's characteristics while contrasting them to the Corinthians' attitude:

> Love is magnanimous, love is kind, is not envious, love does not boast, does not bluster, does not act in an unseemly fashion, does not seek for things of its own, is not irascible, does not take account of evil deed, does not rejoice in injustice, but rejoices with the truth; it tolerates all things,

has faith in all things, hopes in all things, endures all things. *Love never fails.*[89]

In other words: love is all good things and love makes it through everything else to come out on top. Benevolent as it may be, all good things are of God. Because all good things are love. And all love is God. As the great Jewish theologian Abraham Joshua Heschel once wrote, "Nothing stands between God and man."[90] *Nothing.* Because love is the winner. Love is victorious. Nothing stands in its way.

Surveying the Hebrew Bible we see this vision constantly. God is intent on using one family, Abraham's, to bless the entire world.[91] And when Abraham and his descendants fail, God renews God's covenant with Moses, and then with David, and when they fail, too, Godself comes down to show us what the enduring love Paul speaks of is actually like. God let nothing stand in God's way. *Nothing.* Nothing can keep us from the love of God.[92] Because in the end, love is what happens. In the end, love is what *is*. All nations of the world, unconditionally, every single person, will inevitably receive their salvific blessing.[93] Because in the end, there will be only love. A pillar of my faith tradition, Ellen White, once wrote:

> All the springs of tenderness which have opened in the souls of men, are but as a tiny rile to the boundless ocean when compared with the infinite, exhaustless love of God. Tongue cannot utter it; pen cannot portray it. You may meditate upon it every day of your life; you may search the

---

89 1 Corinthians 13:4-8. Emphasis added.

90 Abraham Joshua Heschel, *The Sabbath*, 51.

91 E.g. Genesis 12:2, 22:18.

92 Romans 8:38.

93 M. Eugene Boring, "The Language of Universal Salvation in Paul," *Journal of Biblical Literature*: 282.

Scriptures diligently in order to understand it; you may summon every power and capacity that God has given you, in the endeavor to comprehend the love and compassion of the heavenly Father; and yet there is an infinity beyond. You may study that love for ages; yet you can never fully comprehend the length and the breadth, the depth and the height, of the love of God in giving His Son to die for the world. Eternity itself can never fully reveal it.[94]

Perhaps, then, if love is indeed everything and cannot be understood even in eternity, we underuse the word.

So let me get us started: I love you, Jo—more than eternity itself could ever reveal—and that's why I pissed myself.

---

94 Ellen White, *Testimonies for the Church*, 740.

12

OF BLIZZARD
PROPORTIONS

It doesn't seem like much of anything is eternal. Good meals end. Relationships end. Life ends. Everything comes to a close. But if something is eternal, in my life at least, it is my love for the mountains. Nothing really compares.

I had just begun climbing at places like Smith Rock in central Oregon, and, subsequently, met a couple of dudes, Chad and Tyler, who would both become great friends of mine as we progressed through university together. It was late October, and the leaves had fallen on our college campus. The air was brisk. The local constables had switched out their button-up t-shirts for long-sleeved versions of the uniform. Simply put, we were desperate for something more exciting than pie eating and pumpkin spice sipping.

Having shared ropes and traded belays a few times at our local climbing gym, we were fairly confident in the future of our relationship as climbing partners. One beautiful, clear Friday afternoon we set off to climb, or should I say *hike*, Mount Adams in Washington State. It took us several hours of driving and several more of nighttime hiking, before we reached the peak's infamous "Lunch Counter," where, had we arrived twelve hours earlier, we most certainly would have eaten lunch.

I was pretty tuckered out by the hike in. I had tripped a lot in the snow, so my face was pretty cold, and it was already well past my usual bedtime. On top of that I, for some reason, had packed a heavy climbing rope up with us. It had something to do with my desire to have a "real" mountaineering adventure.

Chad worked with Tyler to set up his granddad's 1980s Mount Everest expedition tent. While they were busy fiddling with the yellow dome, I worked to find the warmest combination of jacket layers I could (as it turns out, cheap fleece and fake Gore-Tex aren't the greatest of combinations). So, as soon as the yellow dome stood ready, I quickly crawled in, zipped up my thirty dollar "zero degree" sleeping bag, and tried to fall asleep. Laying there in between my two new friends, in somewhat of a delirious state, I thought about how strong Chad and Tyler seemed. It wasn't hard to recognize that I had been the one holding the group back on the hike to our nesting ground. I hoped the sleep I was about to partake of would aid me in the forthcoming 1000 meter push to the summit.

Due to our delayed bedtime, no one was out of their sleeping bags until 8 a.m. the next morning—hours later than any seasoned alpinist would ever consider starting their most difficult high-altitude endeavor to date. If my memory serves me correctly, I was the last to raise his head from the sloppily-coiled climbing rope we had used as a pillow, and, subsequently, the last one ready to depart from camp towards the summit. But, as they say, "the last shall be first," so I was indeed the first to raise his ice axe in anticipation of the grand adventure we were all sure to have.

As I lowered my axe, I noticed a large mushroom-shaped cloud was forming over the peak's false summit. During the summer I had paid full-price for a brand-new edition of *The Freedom of the Hills*, the "Bible" of modern mountaineering, in anticipation of my future in the sport. In that particular edition, which I had perused on several occasions, I recalled having seen a photograph of a similarly-shaped cloud over another volcanic summit.[95] It was all too déjà vu to our present situation. Sadly for us, I didn't remember the photo's caption.

Thirty minutes into our hike we were well above our little yellow haven of safety and questing up into what looked like a light snowfall. The mushroom cloud was still well above us, yet we were confident It would pass by the time we reached it. However, it instead chose to reach us. Fifteen minutes later, we were in the thick of it. Visibility was constantly changing from ten meters to only one or two in mere seconds, then suddenly give us the reprieve of an added five or six, only to revert down next to nothing without warning. I feared getting separated from my peers, both of whom were much faster on the uphill, and neglected to pace myself so as to stay within eye and earshot of them in the flurry of white which engulfed us on all sides.

The hike was getting to be far above my pay grade. Each footfall in my mom's old snow boots, the kind with fancy Velcro ankle straps, became closer and closer together. At one point I stopped Chad, who had graciously offered to carry a small rucksack containing all of our personal items, to request my prized Nalgene water bottle. It was the first item I had purchased after I deemed myself "outdoorsy." Its curvy sides were adorned with *valuable* The North Face, Patagonia, La Sportiva, Black Diamond, and Petzl stickers—much to the envy of every half-heartedly outdoorsy guy or gal who came across it. Once Chad passed the pack to me, I opened its elastic topside and reached in for my liter of icy-cold water. As I removed the bottle, Chad said something to the extent of, "Be careful not to let that bottle go, it's icy out here!"

---

95 Ronald Eng, *The Freedom of the Hills*, 556. Seriously though, if you're going to try stuff up in the mountains, read this holy book first. It's worth every penny, even brand-new (but maybe check your local Goodwill first).

Which, as fate would have it, promptly happened.

I let the bottle go, by accident of course, and watched as it plummeted two or three meters down the slope before sliding out of the blizzardy frame. My heart sank. I had a little funeral right then and there for my glissading bottle. Now, both tired and dehydrated, I continued uphill even slower than before.

Chad and Tyler were ahead of me by about five meters when a stiff wind began to blow our way from over the peak's summit. With it came a blinding deluge of spindrift from the mountain both above and around. I so wished we hadn't left the rope sitting comfortably back in the tent, we could have all been tied together, not for safely crossing glaciers, but to be sure that one of us didn't get lost in the whiteout from the rest of the group.

By now the snow was so thick I could barely see my gloved hand held out at an arm's length. We were still about 500 vertical meters from the summit when I realized that I didn't know which way was up or down. I didn't know where Tyler or Chad might be. And, since I didn't have the GPS, I didn't know how to get back to the tent either. Frantically, I leaned down to look for their boot tracks amidst the flurry. Seeing several, I quickly followed them for perhaps fifteen meters before they became too faint to make out any longer. My heart started racing. I assumed I might freeze to death in my little fleece and fake Gore-Tex jackets which were already soaked through.

So, I sat down and waited.

It felt like hours, but I'm sure it was only a couple of minutes before Chad and Tyler came into view. I could barely make out their bright orange and dark blue jackets as they emerged from the blizzardy white torrent. I stood up as they approached and nearly cried from behind the thrifted ski goggles I was wearing.

We took a "summit" selfie there about 500 meters below the true summit, flaunting our ice axes amidst the flaky white background.

We then used Chad's GPS system to advantageously arrive back at our yellow haven of good hope. After considerable confusion as to if the GPS really was right (since it *seemed* like we had come from "that direction"), we arrived at our tent around one in the afternoon—blizzard still raging all around us.

We huddled in the tent together to try and reheat ourselves. My sleeping bag felt like an ice rink beneath my haunches. Chad's beard had frozen over. I couldn't chip the ice off of my camera lens. Even the inside of Tyler's pants somehow had a nice layer of ice which took a while to remove. An hour or so after cramming into the tent, and after wrongly assuming that we could just wait out the storm, we decided to hike back down to the car—blizzard, unused rope, and all.

It took longer than anticipated, but the lower we got on the mountain the more visibility we encountered. As exhausted as we all were, going downhill took far less time than our uphill travels earlier in the day. Yet, we made it to the parking lot and then on to our school's annual Halloween costume competition before dark. Sadly, even dressed as mountaineers, fake Gore-Tex, coiled rope, and all, we didn't win a thing, no matter how realistic our "costumes" may have been.

Now with this story in mind, it would be idiotic of me to think that I am perfect. I mean, my goodness, I got lost in a blizzard! Although my ego has me trending in that narcissistic direction more than I might like, I almost always circle back to the pure lunacy of such thought. Perhaps you can relate.

Paul, in a letter he wrote to some folks in Rome, said, "There is no distinction: for all have sinned and fall short of God's glory."[96] In his context, he's trying to make clear that there is no distinction, culturally, nationalistically, or religiously to whom is subject to sin. Paul, in a way, is simply stating the obvious: sin, the badness all around us, is a universal problem. You cannot escape it and neither can I. Sin is inevitable; it doesn't play favorites. Sin is confusing. It's disorienting. It's scary. It's uncharted. And it, just like a whiteout, all too often has us assume that down is actually up.

The storm we were caught in that October morning was inevitable. It didn't care that Chad had a beard or that Tyler's jacket was orange. Weather reports didn't catch it. And our lack of experience didn't allow us to retreat before starting up the mountain in the first place. We were going to be snared by the blizzard no matter what. And the blizzard didn't care.

But Paul continues. He says that there is hope on the other side of the blizzard, that all are justified freely by God's grace.[97] That's a deal only love can cut. *All are justified freely.* Our role is to just sit down. Wait it out. Do the best you can with what you've got and trust that love will find a way. You may be underprepared. You may be underestimated. You may be misunderstood. But love has got you.

The ancient Israelites seemed to understand this quite well. "In their theology," says John Walton, "something better was coming, though sometimes only after something terrifying."[98] All throughout the biblical metanarrative we see this in play, be it the collective nation or even down on the individual level. Joseph had an oft-lauded story

---

96 Romans 3:22-23.

97 Romans 3:24.

98 John Walton, *Ancient Near Eastern Thought and the Old Testament*, 294.

of such kind, perhaps for good reason. He's sold into slavery by a band of his brothers (something I'm guessing most of us wouldn't wish upon ourselves or anyone else) and is eventually, after many years, in a position to help the very same brothers when he is in power. He could have, justifiably, had his bros sold into slavery—one might say they had it coming. Yet, with incredible grace, he says to them: "Even though you intended to do harm to me, God intended it for good, in order to preserve a numerous people, as he is doing today."[99] Joseph grew out of his own narcissistic ways! The same ways which probably were the root cause of his getting sold into slavery in the first place as his brothers would have seen him as a serious threat to the entire family![100] Somehow God used sin, the nastiness of life, to bring about good—good for everyone in the story.

Yes, sin is terrifying. Sin is inescapable. Sin doesn't play favorites. It's a proverbial virus we're all infected with. But, as Robin Parry points out, it is "an incurable wound that is beyond healing *followed by God's healing*."[101] For love is what heals the painful wound of sin. It's not some top-notch job, a new haircut, or owning a cat who plays fetch. It's a God of love. Truthfully, "God" is but a vernacular abstraction—for love alone is real. Even language like "love" is far too limited to describe what love really is. Human jargon is too finite to describe the infinite. Yet, we must try.

Martin Luther King Jr, in the context of the great American civil rights movement, famously said, "Do to us what you will, and we

---

99 Genesis 50:20.

100 E. Richards & Richard James, *Misreading Scripture with Individualistic Eyes*, 13-14.

101 Robin Parry, "A Universalist View," in *Four Views on Hell*, 114. Emphasis added.

shall continue to love you."[102] If a finite human, as great a man as Dr. King was, can say as much to those who despised and hated him to the point of death, how much more will the infinite God, who we too despised and hated to the point of death, love us through our shortcomings, no matter how grotesque they may be? No matter how much we mess up? No matter how much we suck?

Because the good always follows the bad—love will continue to love you. Invariably. Without doubt. Universally. No questions asked. Forever. Because continued and unconditional love is what heals the wounds of all sin.

So that in the end, there will be only love.[103]

---

102 Martin Luther King Jr, *Strength to Love*, 56.

103 See 1 Corinthians 8:6; John 3:16-17, 16:33; Ephesians 1:19-23.

PART TWO

HOW HUMANITY WAS, IS, AND WILL BE

13

555-KEN

So far in this book, we've talked a lot about God—how God is gracious, how God is good, how God is, if we're going to take scripture and the human experience seriously, only love. In the latter half of *Only Love*, however, we're going to turn our gaze back onto ourselves and who we are in light of a God of love. Because I do believe in a deity in that love is worth our attention, admiration, and worship. As in love is worth emulating. Paul says that "whatever things are true, whatever grand, whatever right, whatever pure, whatever lovely, wherever of good repute—if there be any virtue and be any praise—ponder these things."[104] In other words, think about love—fill your mind— then make your hands busy with love and, there inside of you, you will find God. Because no matter who you are or what you've done, you're made in the image of God, in the image of love.

Personally, I've experienced a lot of love in the vehicular realm. Aside from things like generosity with clutch repairs and having my first kiss in the front seat of my first car, somehow every rig I've ever owned has ended up with a bed in the back.

---

104 Philippians 4:8-9.

My two Toyota sedans have both had their backseats removed so that I could stretch out into the trunk for a nap. Both of these cars have been super cool, too, but as I grew bigger, I wanted something bigger, something better. So, at the beginning of my junior year in college, I procured a van to live in.

It was an old Dodge cargo van which cost me just over a thousand bucks. I bought it from a lady who used to own a tire company up in Washington State. It was one of those pearly white work vans with a roof rack for painting ladders on top and blacked-out windows in the back. The first few weeks with it in my possession were spent insulating the walls as best I could, building a wooden platform for a bed, installing a counter with some shelves, and wiring lines for electricity between a cheap solar panel I had installed on the roof and a small battery inside. I had a big blue jug for water (twenty-seven liters!) and a little red "fridge," better known as a plastic Walmart cooler used to keep my hummus from rotting too fast. I had one of those painting ladders up top for suburban camouflage. I had a coat rack inside and could charge the laptop I used for school straight from the adjacent battery. I even strung a few little lamps from the ceiling to light the space so that I could read at night. It was quite the little setup, even my mom thought it was cool!

Everything was nearly finished when I took the van to the DMV to get a new title and plates. Driving over, I used one of those tapes with an AUX cord in it to play a podcast! This van was tight!

Now I usually like to name the cars I drive. My first car, a red Toyota, was, as you know, christened "Gurdy." Short for Gurtude because she was super old, nearing 500,000 kilometers, and, well, Gurtude isn't a name I've heard bouncing around many preschools recently. The car I have now, a blue Toyota, has the name "Yote" because it's a 'yota. Jo and I got Yote second-hand, and so he's got a nice dent in the rear driver-side door, a weird, black, chipping paint job on the roof, and smells kinda funny when it's cold out. So when I got that new white van, I knew I needed a name for it, too. But it wasn't super old—2003 is pretty darn new for my taste—and it didn't have a bad paint job either; well, at least it wasn't bad after I took a can of white spray paint to it's rust chips. At any rate, I knew I had to pick a name. A good name.

I arrived at the DMV, paid my bill, and received the new title and plates. License plates are usually pretty abnormal and hard to remember, like JAS-796 or SLNK998. But these new plates I was given were different. They read, 555-KEN. Now, I don't really like the number five, or the name "Ken;" it makes me think of a really small, skinny, plastic-looking dude who maybe belongs with a girl named Barbie. But I couldn't help it; the name stuck! I mean, it's like I had gotten custom plates for free!

Not long after christening Ken, I moved in. And after only a few weeks of living in my penny-pinching endeavor, people must have started to notice my decreased awareness of personal hygiene. I was getting offers from folks all over to have me use their showers: friends, co-workers, classmates, professors, heck, even Jo! I wasn't really all that sure if these people meant what they said or not, so I just kept going to the gym showers each day.

My routine was pretty procedural. I would wake up an hour or two before my first class, check both ways out of the van's front window for cops or campus security, get on my rickety old bike, and ride to the gym in sweatpants and a hoodie. People always gave me funny looks as I rode by, especially when I let my hair get long and matted. But I didn't really care, I was keeping myself out of deep debt!

The first time I showered at the gym I had to get used to the boiling hot water beating down on my face and chest since, for some reason, the lever refused to adjust the water's temperature. After overcoming this obstacle using the "jump-in-jump-out" method, I realized I had a new problem: the water wouldn't stay on. It was one of those push-on spigots, hence the lack of heat control. And it would only stay on for five or six seconds at a time, which kind of sucked. So there I was, every morning, hitting the big faucet button as I practiced for the school's annual jumping in-and-out of the shower competition. It was quite the morning workout.

Eventually, after a few weeks of showering at the gym, my friend, Albert, caught wind of my dilemma (or scent) and told me that I was going to shower at his new house for the next month while he and his wife got ready to move in. He had just purchased this new place, pretty close to where I parked my van at night, and insisted I take him up on the offer. Albert even wanted me to sleep there on this big queen size bed. I was reluctant, yet grateful for the hospitality and accepted his garage door opener as a means to get inside the house. Albert really seems to live out his love, not just preach it from the pulpit, and that's always such an awesome thing to watch.

Anyways, early one morning, not long after my conversation with Albert, I snuck out of the van, checking both ways for Officer K, and walked over to the new house. I had decided that sleeping at Albert's place was just too generous of an offer and chose only to shower there when necessary. So, with my shower bag slung over a shoulder, I clicked open the garage door, walked inside, and clicked the door closed behind me.

The house, while new to Albert and his family, was actually pretty old. The floor creaked underneath as I tiptoed towards the bathroom, afraid I might wake the basement renter they had inherited upon purchasing the property. The bathroom door made some unwanted noise, too, and squeaked as I closed it behind me. The washroom itself, which appeared to have been renovated somewhat recently, was equipped with a two-walled tub and a small sink flanked by cabinets on either side. The shower had one of those funny, old-timer, wraparound plastic curtains to prevent spillage. It looked kind of weird, but it sure looked better than practicing for those jumping in-and-out of the shower competitions back at the gym!

Somewhat satisfied with the complimentary accommodations, I did what *almost* all people do when they take a shower.

I got naked.

Like 100 percent naked. It was awesome.

After that vital part of my morning ritual, I stepped into the shower, turned on the spigot, and began to feel the warm water on my chilled feet. A few moments later, I began doing what all good showerers do: I looked for the leaver, the switch, the plug, the button, that thing which has the magical powers to divert the water from the faucet below to the showerhead above!

Sadly, I could not find it.

I knelt down, hunched over in the tub, looking high and low for the magical thing. I looked all around the faucet and the showerhead. I looked inside the tub and even flipped all of the electric switches on the wall trying to make something, anything happen. I gently hit the faucet, only momentarily altering the water's path. I even attempted the trick given to us by our smartphones: I turned it off and then back on again. But to no avail. The water's trajectory simply could not be changed.

With a broken spirit and a heavy heart, I settled for the classic hunchback spit-bath. Folding my nearly two meter frame under the faucet head, I did my best to bathe properly, then dried off and went to class.

A few days later, I got a text from Albert who said that his wife, Allison, had figured the whole shower thing out! All I needed to do was pull down the ring around the faucet to divert the water through the showerhead. What a brilliant fix! I, obviously, would never have thought of such a solution.

Even with the answer in hand, my less-than-fond memories of Albert's shower kept me from returning all that often. I only made the early morning trip once or twice more that month and instead opted to train for the forthcoming shower-hopping competition back at the gym's locker room. Later on, after that month-long move-in period at Albert's place, another couple of friends started letting me use the shower in their apartment. They gave me a key and everything! That was really nice, and because neither of them had spouses, I felt a lot more comfortable about just dropping by to take a shower—especially since their faucet had a normal switch. I did my laundry at their place as well and gave them twenty dollars every now and again as compensation. Things were really looking up, I had my schedule down. Warm showers in the morning and cold shivers in the van at night. It was great! That is until I got caught.

I was packing a bag to leave with Jo for the weekend. We were going to go climbing. The van's doors were wide open to let in the oddly present December sunshine, and I was more than happy to let the van air out after months of nightly habitation.

But then, just as I dropped a duffel bag down from the van's floor onto the concrete below, along came Officer K. *Just kidding!* Along came a representative of campus security. He asked me, in a very suspicious tone, if I was living in my van. I lied and said I lived with my parents (which was true on paper). I was scared that if I told him the truth I would get a fine or something—and, well, I was doing this to *save* money. Sadly, my fears indeed became reality. He acted pretty suspicious of my behavior, and, only a few days later, had put a fat charge on my student account. It was the kind of fine that, if neglected to be paid, would result in my not attending the next quarter.

So, after digging into my honeymoon fund, I paid it. Now, don't be mad I succumbed to the system. I had to pay it to come back the next term! It was my last quarter, and I needed to get that degree! But

I'd be lying if I said I didn't go down without complaining. I even wrote a nice little paper for my privilege and oppression class' unit on socioeconomic inequality; it helped ease the pain a little bit.

Now a lot of people talk about how much pain Jesus was in when he died on the cross. And I'm not one to argue with them—they've written entire books and filmed whole movies on the subject! I just don't think it was the only time in his life where he was uncomfortable or in pain. Like being a carpenter isn't all that bad, unless you stub your sandaled toe on a big plank of wood, or hit your thumb with your hammer instead of that nail you were after. But Jesus must have experienced some pain during his years of homelessness while he was inciting his revolution, too. I mean, he would sleep in parks and crash in his friends' homes. He didn't even have a poorly insulated van to cuddle up in when it was cold out! He was way more homeless than I've ever been. And I'm sure he spent a lot of rainy nights trying to keep himself from getting wet, that is, when he wasn't walking on a big puddle of wetness out to a boat filled with freaked-out disciples.

But what does this kind of lifestyle tell us about Jesus? And perhaps, more importantly, what does it tell us about those who were kind enough to bring him in? What does it mean that Jesus, said to be the ultimate expression of God in the flesh of a human, shivered when it was cold, was sleepy after a long day, got hungry when he hadn't eaten in a while, and thirsty when he didn't have much to drink? He experienced scarcity. He lived in poverty. Yet, he acted like my friends who I just told you about—living his life out of generosity, as though abundance was the norm.

Matthew records Jesus as saying, "I was hungry and you gave me something to eat, I was thirsty and you gave me drink, I was a stranger and you gave me hospitality, naked and you clothed me, I was ill and you looked after me, I was in prison and you came to me."[105] Jesus is doing something really interesting here; in saying this, he's placing God into the shoes of the underprivileged. He's becoming the naked, the sick, the imprisoned. He's saying, "That's me. Now what are you going to do about it?" You see, operating from a mindset of scarcity results in manipulation, fear, violence, anger, and envy. Yet doing what Jesus did and giving of what little we have actually manifests itself as joy, peace, and security. The exact desires which often prompt us to act selfishly. When people treat others like they've got nothing to hold back, they are not just acting on Christ's behalf, *they are Christ*, because that's what God is all about: becoming one in solidarity with us. Jesus is the way, truth, and life in that Jesus gives the clearest representation of a transcendent divine love. But Jesus himself made it clear that he was not the only representation. "Look at the birds," he would say, "Learn of love from them."[106]

A little bit later, Jesus expands his teaching on generosity saying, "I tell you, inasmuch as you did it to one of the least of these my brothers, you did it to me."[107]

Being only love is impossible, friends. I'm not perfect, and I really doubt you are either. We must provide space and allow ourselves to, as Esau McCaulley writes, "mourn our own greed, lusts, and desires that allow us to exploit others."[108] As necessary as that mourning is, our imperfections don't hold us back from being a part of love. Albert was Christ to me in offering to let me sleep and shower at his new

---

105 Matthew 25:35-36.

106 See Matthew 6:26-34.

107 Matthew 25:40.

108 Esau McCaulley, *Reading While Black*, 65.

place. My other friends were Christ to me when they let me sleep on their couch during the coldest of winter nights. You are Christ when you open the door for someone at the store. You are Christ when you comment a kind remark on a friend's Instagram post. You are Christ when you smile and wave at the panhandler on the street corner as you drive by. You and I, *we are Christ!*[109] For love lives in us all. We were born of love. We live in love. *We are love.* We share the same mind, we share the same body, we share the same image, and we have the potential to live our lives out of abundance—knowing that God was, is, and will always be on our side. And that God will, without question, provide us with a way.

Now let me be clear, I'm not asking for your donations so that I can buy a multi-million dollar private jet. I'm no fan of the prosperity gospel, primarily because I know firsthand that living a life with the mindset of abundance and with an attitude of generosity does not mean everything will go well for you. In fact, Jesus, the guy who lived like this 100 percent of the time, was betrayed by one of his closest friends, and was eventually murdered because of it. It won't always be easy. And sometimes I'm scared to be generous because I'm afraid that people will take advantage of my generosity. But then I see Jesus, I see Albert, I see my mom and my dad, I see my wife, I see people who walk into the worst kinds of situations, knowing full well that they will be taken advantage of, *by me*, and yet keep pressing forward because they have chosen a mindset of love over a mindset of scarcity. They understand that love suffers. "God is Love. That is why he suffers," writes Nicholas Wolterstorff, "To love our suffering sinful world is to suffer. God so suffered for the world that he gave up his only Son to suffering. The one who does not see God's suffering does not see his

---

109 1 Corinthians 3:23.

love."[110] God is suffering love. The kind of love that reaches into the deepest hell and redeems.[111]

And if you take a second to look, you'll see that kind of self-sacrificial, generous love all around.

Perhaps even *inside* of you.

---

110 Nicholas Wolterstorff, *Lament for a Son*, 90.

111 Paraphrased from Philip Gulley & James Mulholland, *If Grace Is True*, 68.

14

FOILED KATENAPPING

Before I lived in my car, got myself lost in a blizzard, and pretended not to smell, I was a fetus. And, just like many of you, I didn't know that "fetus" was my status at the time. Now, we all have purpose. I'm a firm believer in that. But I'm pretty sure "baby" isn't the most purposeful of positions to be in. Anyway, when I popped out of my mother, I guess my dad was pretty excited to see me because he quite obviously misspelled my name on the birth certificate. Most Niqs, as you probably know, spell their name like the Christmas saint, "Nick." I, however, have been stuck with a solitary "q" (and no subsequent "u") since 1996. Which, if we're being honest, has been an utter tragedy for anyone who I've ever had to spell my name for.

We were living in Boston, Massachusetts when I began, in earnest, the transition from baby to human. It was in Boston where I was first introduced to the art of talking, as well as the place from where I can recount several of my first memories. They are mostly of big red ladder trucks and orange cargo helicopters, as well as the occasional train conductor or policeman—you know, important stuff.

Before moving to Boston, I didn't really have any friends because, well, most two-year-olds don't have all that many friends. That is except for my cousin, CJ. My mom loves to show me pictures of the two of us kissing. Now personally, I don't really like to see those photos. Because, well, that's incest, and I really don't know how Jo would feel about it. Anyhow, we had moved to Boston from Portland,

Oregon only a few months after I was born. I'm sure the transition was hard for me, what with having to try and find a job and make new friends and all. But I guess CJ made things easier.

I had a birthday just about every year—I think—thank God I wasn't born on leap day. Each birthday I would have the opportunity to try and eat all of the candles on my cake before my father made that *dad-eye-contact* with me. I'm not sure if all toddlers make serious eye-contact in the way I imagine that I did, but I like to think Dad was pretty freaked out due to the intensity of my toddler glare which has only mutated with age causing folks of all kinds to flee for fear of their lives when faced with it.

As it turned out, one birthday I got my present about two months late. It was this weird little human called "Kate." She didn't know it yet, but Kate would eventually grow up to become my sister. For the time being, however, she was just this gross little blob who my mother said I would need to read bedtime stories to. Not that I could read or anything, but I sure did try.

After living in Boston long enough to realize that rooting for the Red Sox, Patriots, Bruins, Pride, and Celtics might get me somewhere in the first twenty-odd years of my life, we moved back to the Northwest. This time to Washington State. There our family grew in size as I gained at least two kilograms every three years. I was so skinny that doctors would interrogate my mother to make sure she wasn't holding back on feeding me. Jo gets the same kind of questions today for some reason. I'm not sure why, though; I'm way fatter than I was in adolescence.

Anyway, in Washington, I started going to school. At home. And like any socially deprived kindergartner, I would run around the house in a "school bus" every morning before class began to make sure the neighbors thought I was crazy.

In the afternoons, my sister and I would get to go play outside. It was a great time. Since I was bigger, stronger, and smarter (or so I thought), I made sure to use my superior size, skill, and wits to demoralize her. One of my favorite ways to do this was to sit high up in a plum tree with a Nerf toy, waiting to blitz on her from above. Camouflage pants and coat, maybe a sandwich, along with a library book detailing the tactics of elite US Army Rangers close at hand. These luxuries were my only friends as I waited in silence to strike. Minutes would go by, sometimes weeks, but I waited nonetheless. I would sit so still I was certain no one could see me. That is, no one except for our dog, Buttercup, who would stand at the base of the tree's trunk, snout pointed skywards, barking her head off for a bite of my sandwich.

I was basically invisible.

One summer day, not long after the Red Sox won their first World Series title in eighty-six years, I was sitting in my perch, with the Nerf toy holstered so that I could take a bite of my sandwich, when I spotted a small pickup truck on the road behind our yard. There was no question I had spotted this particular truck before. Or at least I was pretty sure I had spotted it before. Okay, maybe I hadn't spotted it before. Nevertheless, it was driving by pretty slowly, and I could just make out a face inside peering into our backyard. This shady passing, of course, aroused my junior Army Ranger suspicions.

Kate was running around in the grass, kicking dandelions or something, and Buttercup must have been locked-up in the house because she wasn't begging for my sandwich at the moment. Only a minute later, the very same rig came puttering by again. Yet this time it slowed to a complete stop just outside of our backyard fence.

This was it, this was my time. The moment I had been training so hard for. I mean, *read so much about.*

Slowly, just like on television, I drew my weapon as I set down my sandwich, then re-holstered it because I realized it would be really hard to climb down the tree with only one hand. Soon I was standing on the lowest branch. By this time the driver had one foot hanging out of his truck. I drew the Nerf toy, double-checked to be sure it was loaded with a fluorescent foam dart, and ever-so gracefully leaped onto the ground, firing the projectile in the direction of my sister's sinister stalker.

I doubt the dart made it any more than a meter or two, but my point had been made. The driver looked me square in the eyes, with the same fear and terror I imagine my father had experienced at that birthday party eons ago, and quickly shut his door, speeding away in a hurry. My sister is lucky that I had been reading about Army Ranger tactics! Without all of that book knowledge I might have left the Nerf toy up in the tree! I triumphantly looked back at her and smiled as she, oblivious to the hero I had just become, continued kicking dandelions.

It's amazing how God uses our strange little tendencies for the betterment of others. I didn't know it at the time, but I may have very well saved my sister from getting kidnapped that day! I'm not saying God magically kicked me from the limb so that I could pop into view just as the kidnapper got out of his rig. Instead, I'm saying that the love already in me worked itself into a tangible, yet transcendent, manifestation of what it has always been. God is, even by ancient definition, something that transcends all. Love, the central characteristic of Jesus' new world, is working in us, even when we don't realize it. Because love transcends all. And it's always working to make a difference for the betterment of the whole. Working to keep little sisters safe. Working to fill what was once empty. Paul seemed to be on the same page when he talks about the body of Christ:

> For—just as the body is one and has many members, yet all the members, while being many, are one body—so also the Anointed ... God has situated the members, each one of them, in the body as he has willed. And if all were one member, where the body? Yet now, in fact, many members but one body.[112]

You see, friends, speaking from the Christian perspective, as tainted as it may be from the likes of Augustine, the piety of the Middle Ages and the often repulsive nature of modern fundamentalism, we are *all* a part of this greater whole.[113] And while my part may be tasked with scaring away potential kidnappers with Nerf toys, you may have been constructed to be a TV personality, or a softball player, or a granddad. We are one body, yet you may be an eye while I am a few cells off to the left side of the liver! We are not the same. In fact, we are very different! We each have a purpose, a niche if you will. Paul is pointing us towards what God in us really looks like, a combination of both diversity and unity.[114] For we are not all perfectly alike, and expecting us to look the same, act the same, and think the same denounces the creativity of the Creator.

Too often I get caught up comparing myself to others, "I make five-figures, and she makes seven!" Or, "I'm vegan, but he's just vegetarian." The problem with this is that when we get caught up in these kinds of conversations, and all of us do, we lose sight of the greater love already in place. We must stop looking to the sky as our ancestors

---

112 1 Corinthians 12:12, 18-20.

113 See Krister Stendahl, "The Apostle Paul and the Introspective Conscience of the West," *Harvard Theological Review*: 200.

114 John Muddiman & John Barton, *Oxford Bible Commentary*, 117.

have for millennia, longing for our savior to come, and instead look to the love all around us and see that God is already here, alive in the goodness we all espouse. Sometimes we simply forget that we are a part of this grander vision, something far bigger than ourselves. We forget that love works in ordinary people like us to get extraordinary things done. Meaning that all of us ordinary parts, collectively, are this great and wondrous body of Christ, and that love is not the body's duty, but instead its collective *destiny*.

We are what makes the creator a creator—for without her art, the artist does not exist.

Humor me for a second here, but if we were to take Paul's analogy one step further, we've got to realize that the body is made of parts that are never meant to cross paths. If, proverbially, you're an eye and I'm a liver, we may never see each other! (If we ever did come into contact something would be very wrong with the body.) We are all different parts, yes. We all have different roles to play, of course. And we may all be moving differently, but, and this is important, we are moving together. Similar trajectory. Same intentionality. In solid perpetuity. As parts of the body of love we are moving differently, *together*.

That's only love. Diversity is our strength and because of that, radical inclusion must be our song. Not just in the color of our skin, or our hair, or our flag, but also in our beliefs and creed. We must believe, as Huston Smith writes, that "the whole is invariably better than the sum of its parts."[115] Because, if we're honest, nobody's got the entire pie when it comes to the ways of love.

---

115 Huston Smith, *The Soul of Christianity*, 7.

For several years after the foiled "Katenapping" as I like to call it, I had serious nightmares about being kidnapped. I remember waking up in the middle of the night, cold sweat and all, hopping out from under the covers to go over to my bedroom window and check to be sure it was locked. These days I don't have as many nightmares, but I do keep a Nerf toy under my pillow while I sleep—you just never know when you might need one.

15

THE BUGABOO BUG

I had been bit. And it hurt.

No, it wasn't in a nightmare. Because, come springtime several years ago, I received a text from a group chat that had become surprisingly dormant. The message itself was unmistakably a hyperlink that I clicked, which magically took me to an online video. The clip wasn't more than three minutes long, but that's all the time I needed to get bit. Bit by the Bugaboo bug.

The video featured tall granite spires poking out of sweeping white glaciers. Clear blue skies above them. And no precipitation whatsoever. I nearly broke down into tears, the vista was just that breathtaking—even viewed on the tiny screen of my mobile phone.

I had only been climbing for about a year at this point in life. However, the wretched combination of cragging one weekend then slogging up blizzardy volcanos the next, was no longer speaking to my soul in the way it had a few months prior. But this, what I was looking at on my cell's screen, this was different. Something bigger. Something better. Something life-giving.

Sixteen months and two failed trip attempts later, I drove Gurdy from a completed summer gig in central Oregon to a spot along the Puget Sound just north of Seattle, Washington. There I was met by two of my climbing partners and dearest friends, Chad and Tyler. Both of whom had spent the summer in one of the most miserable of ways imaginable: studying biology.

Rounding off our regular group of climbing chaps was the rookie, the young gun, the punk wiener, Al. Now Al just happens to be the brother of Chad, a modern-day Sasquatch hunter who has traveled the world over in search of exotic Bigfoots. Tyler also decided he ought to come along. And, being that he had just passed a test to be certified as a single pitch climbing instructor by the American Mountain Guide Association, we figured we could use a "professional" guide for the forthcoming expedition. The pure professionalism of Tyler's guiding habits were in full array during the twelve-hour drive to Canada, as he was tasked with driving all twelve of the hours. It was a fabulous deal for the rest of us. As was customary on long road trips with this particular crew, episodes of popular climbing podcasts began to mix with Latin pop hits. Malcolm Gladwell's voice began to blend with Frank Sinatra's jazzy tunes. Even the obnoxious snoring of our resident Sasquatch hunter began to blend beautifully with the rumblings of our stomachs. The occasional stop at Tim Horton's, along with frequent stops at public washrooms (once we had migrated north of the border), made for plenty of opportunities to stretch our legs during the extended drive.

After what seemed like at least a half-day of driving, we arrived at the trailhead. The trailhead to the Bugaboos! Three of us seemed pretty well-rested and wanted to get ourselves, along with our many kilos of "necessary" gear, up to Applebee Dome where we would set up a base camp. However, our "guide" seemed a bit more tuckered-out than the rest of us. So, we just bedded-down right there in the parking lot, risking an attack from some of the local porcupines and grizzly bears we had passed on the drive in. Let me be real with you for a second … it took a lot of courage to fall asleep that night.

Because of our restless sleep, waking up the next morning was nothing short of dreadful. There was this big light coming from the sky and movement all around the parking lot from other climbers getting ready to begin their hike up to basecamp. It was also pretty chilly out, and I was nearly naked, covered only by my sleeping bag. I sleep naked most nights in the backcountry because I want to be as light as possible should I need to outrun my friends in the event of a bear attack. However, I am happy to report that we weren't attacked by any critters that night, large or prickly. That being said, I wasn't exempt from struggling to pull on a pair of my pants while attempting to remain covered by my sleeping bag. I eventually overcame the obstacle and proceeded to find out how the other fellas had fared in their attempts at waking up. Chad and Al were already awake, sipping coffee and calling for a Sasquatch to join them around their camp stove. Tyler only needed a gentle prodding to exit his cocoon that particular morning as he, like the rest of us, was beyond excited to hike in, set up camp, and begin climbing.

We ate, packed up our bags, drank a few last gulps of bacteria-free water, locked our car's doors, and hit the trail. Al, a Boston Marathoner, quickly took the lead, with the remaining three of us in cold pursuit, but he was also our resident rookie in the climbing scene and didn't have a proper alpine climbing pack. So his brother, being the kind-hearted individual that he is, offered Al his 150 liter duffel bag as a backpack—the kind yaks and donkeys carry as porters into the most remote mountain regions of the world. Minimal shoulder cushion. No waist strap. No back support. All to be carried up a trail with just over 1000 meters of elevation gain in less than five kilometers distance. Al was already epicing.

After an hour and a half of sustained suffering, "Mr. Lite Pack" (yours truly) made it to the Canadian Alpine Club's famed Kain Hut, sitting only a couple hundred meters below Applebee Dome where we intended to set-up camp. I had passed young Al quite some time before and, being the first to arrive at this milestone thanks to increased mobility from my limited pack weight, sat down and waited for the rest of the boys to saunter in. I unpacked my bag, ate a bar, chatted with a few of the local chipmunks, and soaked up the sunshine. It was quite the relaxing event. Eventually, the rest of the crew showed up and we made our way to the dome, unpacked all of our gear, and set up our tents.

Upon the completion of our unpacking procedure, Tyler, although obviously quite tired from his ascent up into the alpine area, decided it would be in the group's best interest to climb something that very day. While we were all fairly gung-ho to the idea of climbing, since we had indeed hiked all of that way to climb things, we weren't entirely certain as to the time. Being that we didn't quite know the time, we weren't sure how much daylight was left to climb. Now just to be clear, we all had phones, watches, and plenty of other gizmos and gadgets which were created to tell time. However, they all appeared to have joined in cahoots against us, as each device had chosen a different time zone to display. Needless to say, we were very confused. Eventually, we decided that we probably ought to run up something easy. Something not very technical. Something super fun. Something short enough to beat the soon-to-be setting sun.

The west ridge of Pigeon Spire, a classic introductory Bugaboo route, seemed to be the perfect objective. We only wasted a few more minutes of precious daylight to bicker about who should be partnered with who. Eventually, it was decided that the tall, skinny kid who used to live in Boston, would be paired with Al, the fit kid who had just run the Boston Marathon. I could feel it in my bones—this was going to be a great time.

We packed-up our climbing ropes, shoes, and hardware, and headed out of camp. We then crossed a large boulder field before making our way up the Snowpatch-Bugaboo Col, a steep snowbank situated between two large rock towers. About halfway up, Al and I became *super* grateful to a large guided party above us for making our ascent up the col a memorable occasion. As the inexperienced among them rappelled down, there were several rocks, some the size of softballs, which whizzed by our heads. As you can imagine, we were absolutely stoked at the opportunity to play an impromptu round of alpine dodgeball that afternoon.

Thankfully, the two of us made it up to the top of the col without physical ailment. We roped up and worked our way across a crevasseless glacier to the base of Pigeon Spire's western ridge. Al, the marathon runner, happened to do a bit better than I as far as speed was concerned. However, being that we were roped up, I was lucky enough not to let him get too far ahead of me! Several times I did have to employ different excuses as to why I couldn't exactly sprint up the hill as he was attempting to do: "Oh, you know, I just tore my MCL a few months back and she's getting mighty sore, so just give me a minute to let me do a few of the stretches my physical therapist taught me!" or, "Hey so look over there at that beautiful rock formation, let's just stand here for a second and soak in its beauty because, I mean, it's such a beautiful rock!" or, "Wow, look how far ahead of Chad and Tyler we are, that's so great, we're so fast; we're doing a fabulous job, really. Maybe we should slow down to let them catch up?" or the classic, "Hey stop right there, I need to get my camera out; you look so cool standing right there—this is going to be one great photo! You're not going to regret having this to post on Instagram!"

I suppose Al could have made it to the base of the rock route in record time, that is if it wasn't for me and all my devious slow-down tactics. Not to mention that we deviated from our direct course to go and pin down someone's little green tent, which had been blowing around for who knows how long, in the middle of a glacier off to our right. Nonetheless, we eventually made it to the massif, sat down, swapped out our stiff rubber boots for soft climbing shoes, drank some fresh glacier water, quickly racked up, and began to climb.

It was easy scrambling pretty much the entire way to the summit. No crazy moves—it was like climbing a massive ladder with perfect granite rungs. Even though Al and I had brought along a rope, we opted to move fast and simply solo the entire route. The freedom of soloing combined with the easy grade and effortless moves, all amid the absolutely glorious expanse that is the Bugaboos, made for an entrancing experience. The Bugaboo bug had bitten, and I was totally fine with it.

Soon, we topped out on the summit and set up our rope to rappel; then descended the summit block to a small saddle where we met the ascending duo of Chad and Tyler. We shared high-fives, posed for some photos, and said we were looking forward to meeting again for dinner back at camp.

The next morning we all awoke at the leisurely hour of nine. Actually, it could have been ten, maybe even eleven (remember, our clocks were in cahoots against us). Talking over dinner the night before, we had hoped to get a good alpine start on our day's adventure, but maybe that wasn't in the best interest of our bodies. Or, as Chad often says, "If we start a few hours after everyone else does, we'll have the popular routes all to ourselves!"

We bickered again, as all climbers do, about which classic route to send that day. We questioned, too, if it was simply too late to do anything but run circles around our tents and then wait to send something big and classic early the next morning. Since we only had that day and the next before we needed to head back down to the car and then to the States, we opted to climb the ultra-classic northeast buttress of Bugaboo Spire that very afternoon.

Again, Al and myself were paired, as were Chad and Tyler. We set off sometime around noon, give or take an hour depending on whose clock you looked at. After heading past some local ice-cold lakes created from spring snowmelt, we crossed another crevasseless glacier, skipping the rope-up this time around, and made our way to a short wall which we would use to climb to the saddle situated at the base of Bugaboo Spire. We racked up, put our boots and axes in our backpacks, and began to scramble to the top of the saddle so as to reach the base of the afternoon's climb.

Tyler, our professional guide, led the charge with Chad in tow. While he was working on the first pitch's lieback, Al and I chatted about the weather, some dark clouds off to the north, and how late it was getting—already like two or three in the afternoon. We talked about how we had heard it often storms during summer afternoons in the Bugaboos, and how folks don't recommend being caught up high when they hit (since keeping your life attached to reality by only a few bits of metal and millimeters of fabric is not the safest of options in an electric storm). We ate a granola bar or two as we sat there. I distinctly remember offering to share some of my food with Al, so as to butter him up, since I knew I would need to ask him a favor as I was to lead all ten pitches of technical rock. But when I finally worked up the nerve to pop the question, it went off far better than I had imagined:

"Hey, Al?"

"Yeah."

"Hey, so what if you take two of my boots in trade for one of yours?"

"Sure."

Long pause.

"And my ice tool as well?"

"Sure thing."

What a great guy, right? Now to a five-year-old, this deal may very well sound phenomenal: I mean he received three of my things in exchange for just one of his! But when you are brand-spanking new to big traditional multi-pitches, as Al was, this is actually a pretty crappy deal. Because all it does is add weight to his backpack and he doesn't even get to permanently keep the bonus boot and extra ice axe as compensation! But, Al, being the Boston Marathoner he is, followed all ten pitches of the climb with three boots and two axes in his pack like a champ—*a champion's champ.*

The climbing again was phenomenal. The granite, of an absolutely fabulous quality. Certainly a classic. Al and I crested the north summit at around 7 or 8 p.m. The winds had picked up considerably and the dark clouds we had seen earlier, while sharing a snack below, were collecting right above our heads. We tried to make quick work of getting ourselves over to the south summit, where Tyler and Chad were waiting for us, as we had planned to use both parties' ropes for the descent. Sadly, several miscommunications between the four of us resulted in my rappelling an extra ten meters off of the north summit, setting Al and I back considerably. And, seeing that we would be a while, Chad and Tyler began the descent on their own.

After I ascended the rope back up to where I should have stopped originally, Al came down to join me and we both traversed to the south summit where we were to begin our descent. During our long drive into the Bugaboos, I was reading that descending this particular side of the mountain after dark, when you hadn't climbed it before, could lead to an unexpected overnight bivy (or two!) due to its maze-like nature. While I'll admit that our route down was indeed confusing on occasion (thankfully not to the extent that we needed to hastily improvise a mountainside campsite), Al and I were mostly frustrated with the number of times our rope got caught when we pulled it down after a rappel. One time the rope was caught so firmly that Al had to climb up at least ten meters of vertical rock, without protection, 400 meters off the deck, to retrieve the darned thing from its wedged outcropping! Now, I've gotten a lot of ropes stuck while climbing before. But never before have I had such a terrible experience! It seemed as though one of us had to climb up and untangle the darned thing at just about every-other rappel. We both screamed at the sky several times. We banged our (helmeted) heads against the rock a few times too. And, to make matters worse, just as we noticed the lights from Chad and Tyler's headlamps emerge on the flat ground far below us, the wind picked up, and it started to pour a strange mixture of sleet and snow onto our already chilled bodies.

With our hoods now up and heads down, we finished our last few rappels, and began running, in our tight rubber rock shoes, down the trail to the top of Bugaboo-Snowpatch Col, the same place we had played alpine dodgeball the day before. We rapped two or three times more to get off of the snow slope and down onto the glacier below. By this time it was nearing two in the morning (although it could have been one or three; again, our clocks), and Al and I wanted nothing more than sleep. Long. Hard. Beautiful sleep.

As we began to slowly saunter back to camp, through the boulder fields and up the steep trail to the top of Applebee Dome, the snow transformed into pounding rain. We soon were running towards our campsite. During our jog, we noticed a few other climbers already up and packing for their early alpine starts. We were proud of them, but were both pretty thankful to have gotten back to our tents and off the peak before the storm rolled itself in on us full-force!

Come morning, all four of us awoke at different times: Chad woke up to yawn once or twice, then rolled over and, no jokes here, stayed in his sleeping bag until early the *next* morning when we were packing up to leave camp altogether. Al woke up about an hour after we got into our tents to go run a marathon or something (that is a joke, *I think*). Tyler, as always, was pretty stoked on sleeping late, too, but got up and made himself breakfast around midday. I woke up only once or twice before noon to take a pee in my Gatorade bottle, before getting out of bed to make some noodles for lunch before walking down to the creek, just below our campsite, to try and take an alpine bath.

The day was obviously going to be a rest day—with no real climbing whatsoever.

We ate a whole lot. I crammed so much food down my esophagus that I was asking the other guys, all of whom had hauled obnoxious amounts of food up from the parking lot, if they had anything extra to share. Somehow I haggled my way into a free box of rice (thanks again, Al!), and some raisins (thanks, kind of, Chad). Everyone but Chad, who yawned the day away, ran up Eastpost Spire, just a stone's throw from our campsite, at one point or another. I also tried to solo some hand crack just to the right of our tents but got scared at the crux and spent nearly twenty minutes backing down. Tyler and Al, "Mr. Guide Guy" and "Mr. Safe Dude" respectively, later set up a toprope on the crack and had a good time actually climbing it in its entirety. We all just chilled. It was great.

It was great until I realized that this was to be my last day in the Bugaboos. We needed to leave the next morning so as to get back for some other engagements we had in the "real" world. I was pretty disappointed, only one real climb for a heck of a lot of hiking? That's a bum deal. But then again, that one climb was pretty great indeed.

We awoke around five (or six, or four) the next day, and headed back down into the valley. The Bugaboos are a beautiful place, a really *special* place. I've never been anywhere so beautiful, and I've never had such a good time bickering with folks about the time either! It's been years since I was last there in the flesh, but the Bugaboo bug still seems to have infected me. I can't tell you how many times my mind has wandered to the Bugs right before bed, while in the shower, or when on a run. Beautiful places seem to do that. They call me. They toy with my imagination, begging me to come play in them once again.

- ♡ -

Beautiful spaces have this intrinsic ability to beckon us. All of us. And I think that's because they don't care what color your skin is, and they don't care what language you might speak. Beautiful spaces don't care which church you go to or in which direction you pray. Beautiful spaces don't care who you voted for in the last election or how much you had to drink last night. Because beautiful spaces are just that—they are *beautiful*. Non-judgemental. How could they be anything different?

They are perfect, and perfectly content, in their imperfections. Beautiful in their blemishes. It is their flaws that create their beauty. The raging river which carves the canyon. The ever-moving glacier which shapes mountain peaks. And these beautiful, unbiased spaces are all around us. All of the time. Even when we can't see them. When we're blinded by the mess of life. When we're shackled by the imperfections and fears of the journey. Even when we can't see at all because of the darkness all around, they are there, calling us to come join in their beauty. Because creation itself is an act of love.[116]

I've spent much of this book talking about how it is God who is only love. How it is God who is gracious. How it is God who is good. And that is oh so true, but this good God says something about you and about me. God says that we are good too—God wants all of us to recognize the love we are created to be. God made us of Godself to be a part of Godself. The centerpiece of creation, made to be creators.[117] The God of love, the God of creation, created you to love. Humanity is meant to create only love. Humanity is good. Humanity is beautiful. And we are all a part of this cosmic goodness, created to

116 As pointed out by Clark Pinnock in, "An Inclusivist View," in *Four Views on Salvation in a Pluralistic World*, 103.

117 See John Walton, Victor Matthews, & Mark Chavalas, *IVP Bible Background Commentary: Old Testament*, 28.

create more of it. Not through judgement of those unlike ourselves but through embracing the perfection of our imperfections. For we are all a part of love.

Honestly, religion is the root of so much of the evil we see in the world; since the dawn of humanity it has spent time crafting boundaries that separate the love we all are. Things like religion, politics, and oppressive economics have all torn the body of love apart. For when a religion creates gods who dehumanize the "other," the beauty of our imperfections is often translated into muck and mire. I wonder how one of the most anti-religious fanatics, Jesus, would feel knowing we created yet another religion in his name. Rather than living *in, through, and as* Christ, which is perhaps the most humanizing of all acts, we Christians have resorted to living *for* Christ—as one lives for a popular politician or movie star. We've only gone so far as to slap a bumper sticker on our truck or plant a campaign sign in our yard espousing our support for God. Yet a God of love cannot be contained by simple support. Because love transcends—love is beyond what we can conceptualize, therefore, it is beyond what we can compartmentalize.

This love I'm talking about isn't simply for those who we humans deem as being "worthy" of it. For justice, in the human system, is merely an abstraction of whomever is in power. Justice in the power structure of grace, however, says that love is for all—*because it is all.* Love is not exclusive to any one person, building, church, denomination, gender, skin color, sexual orientation, country, or religion—*because it is in all of them.* Love is not just our potential, it is our reality. It is the beauty which permeates all things, moving in and through us—*because it is us.* You are perfect in your imperfections. Beautiful in your blemishes. It is your flaws, *your sin,* which prove your perfection.

What I'm about to say may prove blasphemous or heretical, but God seems keen in having us join God in God's divinity. Psalm 82 is a really interesting examination of an oft-forgotten biblical theme where the imperfect are somehow still divine:

> God has taken his place in the divine council; in the midst of the *gods* he holds judgment: "How long will you judge unjustly and show partiality to the wicked? Give justice to the weak and the orphan, maintain the right of the lowly and the destitute. Rescue the weak and the needy; deliver them from the hand of the wicked." They have neither knowledge nor understanding, they walk around in darkness; all the foundations of the earth are shaken.[118]

So, it sounds like there are some gods who have messed up. They've shown partiality to evil things, and God is attempting to persuade them to instead become partial to practical goodness, mercy, and love. If we're going to be honest with ourselves, this sounds a whole lot like the current state of our planet, where the weak and needy, the collective, are neglected for the sake of others' individual gain. The author goes on, speaking to the gods, quoting the voice of God, and says: "You are gods, children of the Most High, all of you."[119]

We later see Jesus quote this line when talking to some Jewish leaders who were furious at some of his assertions regarding divinity.[120] He uses it in such a way that asserts his accusers, humans, were the "gods" spoken of in the psalm. Meaning that in the eyes of God, *humans are divine.* As maimed and blind as we may be, we still bear the image of God, the image of love. We are perfect in our imperfections; for when God looks at us, love is all that God sees.

You are only love—even when you can't see it.

You are only love—because you were made in its image.

---

118 Psalm 82:1-5. Emphasis added.

119 Psalm 82:6.

120 John 10:34-36.

16

SLEEPLESS IN SEATTLE (AND UTAH)

Because I was homeschooled during my early years, I often had the freedom to rearrange my day as I saw fit, just so long as assignments and various chores were through by nightfall. Because of such freedom, I became an obsessive reader. Pouring over books for hours at a time. I once read all seven books of C.S. Lewis' *Narnia* series in under twenty hours—on a school day, no less. I didn't sleep much that night, but it was worth it. A couple of years ago, Jo got a hold of a pre-release copy of one of my favorite author's newest books, and it took me six weeks to read. *Six weeks!* I finished reading it the day before the book actually came out for public sale. I have no idea how thirteen-year-old Niq could come along and read a collection of books four times as long, cover-to-cover, just over the morning's coffee!

Maybe it's because I didn't care as much about sleep back then. But these days, I guess you could say I enjoy sleeping. Sleeping late. Taking naps. Going to bed early. They're all great! Sometimes, I do sacrifice my sleep here and again to stay up late. Mostly when I'm writing, say this book, for instance. And while it's not as enticing anymore, swimming used to persuade me to avoid Pastor Pillow for a couple of extra hours, too.

During that particular phase of my existence, I attended a conference in Seattle, Washington. While there, I ran across a friend of mine,

Noah. We had met close to five years prior, while in Central America, and had kept in touch since. One of my first memories of Noah is how the two of us braved local jellyfish to take a late-night dip off the coast of Belize. So when the first day of presentations at the conference were over, we decided to make our way down to the Puget Sound and keep the tradition alive.

Noah knew the town a little better than I, so he took point. The building where the gathering was being held sat only a kilometer or two away from Seattle's famed Space Needle. So, we made our way there, hoping to get a bird's-eye view of things from the high ground. Sadly, the security guards wouldn't let us any further into the tower than the gift shop—something about everything being already reserved because of Valentine's Day. Our failure to reach the needle's observation deck didn't phase us though, as we eventually found a vacant parking garage nearby, from the top of which we could see the sound's water reflecting city lights all around. It didn't appear to be too far away, so we decided to run. Down several streets, by apartment buildings and corner convenience stores, even past a toddler on one of those plastic trikes! After several minutes, we arrived at the edge of a busy five-lane street. Across from the street stood a tall chain-link fence. On the other side of that fence, a railyard, and, past the railyard, the sound itself.

After crossing the road, we realized that there had to have been at least eight or nine sets of tracks between us and the saltwater we craved. So, as best we could, we closed our eyes while climbing around signs which read "No Trespassing" and scaled the fence. Next, we had to dodge in and out of boxcars. It kind of felt like we should be in some kind of video game, except, well, we didn't have any extra lives to spare were we to get crushed by one of the iron monsters.[121] We then hopped over another fence and were confronted with the most beautiful of nighttime sights: lights from nearby oil tankers flickering on the water's surface.

We moved down onto the beach and made a local piece of drift-wood our basecamp for the forthcoming adventure. It was cold out that night—February in the Northern Hemisphere has that way about it—and, once we had made it out from amongst all of the city's buildings, the brisk wind really didn't help much either. We then discovered that we had neglected to bring along a towel, and, for a moment, I think neither of us really wanted to go through with our original plan.

But, as young machismo often does, we hyped each other up enough to start taking our clothes off. First came the shoes. Socks next. Then sweaters and hats. Followed by our shirts. We were hesitant to pull off our pants and undergarments. The lights from the oil tankers in front and city behind us illuminated our pale white skin quite nicely. I recall asking Noah, "Wouldn't that be funny if some couple on a romantic stroll walked by on the path? I mean, it is Valentine's Day." We both laughed, nervously, and assured each other that something like that couldn't happen. It was too late at night. Everyone was already in bed!

With a sudden burst of adrenaline, after stripping off the remainder of my attire whilst charging for the water, I yelled, "Cannonball!" and jumped. As I neared submersion I noticed movement out of the corner of my eye. The motion came from just behind the driftwood Noah and I had been sitting on. As my bare feet touched the frigid

---

121 I may have hyped this up a bit too much—the boxcars weren't moving or anything, in fact, the entire railyard was eerily quiet. But we still felt pretty badass.

water, I turned around to look behind me and realized that the movement I had seen was that of a human. Yet, it wasn't Noah. It wasn't a local policeman (thank God it wasn't Officer K). And it certainly wasn't a mirage. For rising from a bush behind our driftwood was what I assume had to have been a homeless gentleman.

I was half-way into the water at this point and, as such, was maybe ten meters away from Noah and our new companion. I froze, both literally and in the figurative sense of the word, as my genitals became submerged in the sound. It was then, as he began to run, that we made some all too confrontational eye contact.

I was already too committed to completing my dip, so I closed my eyes and fully immersed myself in the frigged saltwater sound. My hair was long and flowy at that point in life, so I was sure to wet every strand (otherwise, it wouldn't have counted as a true dip and I would have needed to return to the unpleasant environment). As my head burst back through the water's threshold, I wiped the hair and water out of my eyes and opened them. To my left floundered Noah, midway through the process of his dunk. And off to my right, still running, was the poor chap whose name I'll never know.

I doubt he'll ever forget that late-night Valentine's experience. He was trying to sleep, but two kids showed up, sat next to his bunk, stripped themselves bare, and ran into the water screaming, "Cannonball!" I'd be scared out of my wits if that ever happened to me.

I suppose precious sleep is sometimes worth losing out on so as to avoid such a memorable vista.

- ♡ -

My friend Mason, however, has a different take on circadian rhythms.

Mason is a great guy. Hardworking. Energetic. Bright. A true joy to be around. Because of those characteristics, he makes a great partner for lots of different adventures. We first met in high school. He was trying to make the basketball team, as was I. He made it. I didn't. We had a few classes together as well. He always seemed to get the high A's, while I settled for a lower version of the grade. We even spent some time in college together. He enrolled in a rigorous engineering curriculum, and I in a program far more religious in nature. We also worked together at a youth camp in northern Idaho for a couple of summers. As you might have guessed, he was pretty great at summer camp, too. Each day he would remind me of how good a swimmer he was when, during our lunch break, I'd be panting to keep up with him while swimming laps in the lake. Over the years we've also taken a few road trips together where we would climb, run, kayak, camp, or go canyoneering. He's one of those friends you're really excited to get a phone call from, because, well, he's just a really great guy. Needless to say, I've always enjoyed having him around, that is, until one fateful spring morning.

We had just driven all night, from southeast Washington to southwest Utah. Mason and I were in a car with Tyler and Jo. The four of us had gotten along splendidly as we drove through the night. We sang songs, shared stories, and snacked on snacks. You know, classic road trip stuff.

It was about 5 a.m. when we dropped Jo off at a rural desert airport so that she could fly home to visit her folks. The rest of us, however, were going to stay behind and climb some local limestone for the week. Sleepily, Tyler drove the car to a patch of public land just outside of town. As soon as he had parked, I quickly exited the vehicle, threw my foam pad out onto the reddish-clay ground, and cuddled up inside my sleeping bag for a good morning's sleep.

As I zipped up my jacket and covered my eyes with a beanie, I thought, *Finally, after thirteen hours of trying to stay awake so as to keep Tyler awake while he was driving, I get to sleep.*

What seemed to happen only moments later will forever be ingrained in my mind.

A voice, faint at first but which gained volume at an aggressive rate, filled the crisp air around me. I rolled over, trying in earnest to extinguish the violently dreadful sound—but to no avail. Eventually, after removing the hat from my eyes and unzipping my sleeping bag and jackets, I began to realize the horrid voice was that of my good friend, Mason. He was pacing back and forth, between my bivy spot and Tyler's car—I suppose to release some pent-up "energy" from the thirteen-hour car ride we had finished only three hours before—shouting at the top of his lungs.

"Niq, wake up!" he yelled in *somewhat* of a playful voice, "It's time to go climbing!"

My eyes, unaccustomed to the ever-growing luminesce of the sun, wandered, looking for Mason or at least his shadow. I picked up a clump of hard clay and threw it in what I thought was the direction of my perpetrator but was actually Tyler's newly-acquired Honda CRV.

Again, Mason's voice pierced my ears with his, "Wake up, guys, it's time to go!" followed by, "I'm so bored right now, c'mon guys, wake up!"

Much to both my and Tyler's chagrin, this playful exchange continued for the next *two hours.*

Mason would be silent for several minutes, then, just as the promise of sleep had begun to turn into something more concrete than a fleeting wish, speak up again. We had all gone to bed at 6 a.m. and I simply could not fathom why Mason wanted Tyler and myself up at 9:30! I mean, How was he even this wide awake? He hadn't slept on the drive either!

After throwing all of the rocks and clay clumps within an arm's reach of my bedroll, I finally gave in and let him talk unchallenged. And, for the remainder of our weeklong trip, I plotted. I wanted to make Mason a cup of coffee one morning, lace it with some crushed melatonin sleeping pills, then keep him awake by yelling about how much I wanted him to stop being sleepy so that we could go climbing! (The bottle said that the supplements were natural, so I wasn't worried about killing him or anything.) I also considered putting a cactus or two dozen down into the bottom of his sleeping bag so as to irritate his little toes before bed. Both of those options seemed too harsh, so I instead settled with reminding him of his waking-Niq-up *mistake* on an hourly basis for the remainder of our trip.

It wasn't until several years later, and after lots of reflection, that I came to appreciate Mason's vehemence. His passion. His persistence. His zeal for getting a move on that morning. This isn't to deny my utter dissatisfaction with him in the moment, as it did seem as though Mason had nary a care for my sleeping habits, but as time has progressed, my perspective has shifted. Mason chose not to walk in the limitations which he had been handed. He isn't just like this with sleep, either. Mason climbs, cycles, runs, studies, works, and even eats with everything he has. My friend Mason lives a full life because he has chosen not to be limited by the imperfections around and inside of him.

There is a peculiar freedom that comes with living in such a way. Mason has chosen to consume his life and, more often than not, avoid letting his life consume him. Mason lives his life out of love. Not because he's pious or super religious or anything like that, but because he knows that everything has a habit of working out, perhaps not always in his best interest, but always for the betterment of the whole in the end, when he chooses to love intentionally. It's not often you find people like that—people who live out their love intentionally and aren't limited by the singular path most people see. Somehow they see bigger than what's right in front of them, knowing that there are always forks ahead. They see through the mire and cling to what is good.

In the Hebrew Bible, this guy named Jeremiah gets tossed into a muddy underground dungeon.[122] I'm sure it wasn't anywhere near as cold as the Puget Sound that night during Noah and my Valentine's dip, but it was probably a lot dirtier. Anyway, he gets chucked into the cistern and a foreigner hears about it. An Ethiopian named Ebed-melech. And Ebed-melech, the foreigner, goes and rounds up thirty guys to yank the now very muddy Jeremiah out of the pit. Ebed-melech wasn't in a position of power or anything like that. In fact, as a non-Isrealite, he probably didn't have much of a say in much of anything, but when he saw someone in need, he made the difference. He knew he could do something good, and he persisted until that good thing came to fruition. He knew he was free to do good and wasn't about to wait around for permission to do it.

Louie Giglio says at the end of his book, *Goliath Must Fall*, that "Jesus is already victorious. Now is the time to walk in the freedom that he has won."[123] Take a moment to let that sink in: *love has already won*. And love's big win calls us into action. It calls us to walk in the freedom that only love can provide.[124] Because God is nothing more and nothing less than love. The love we see freely given all around us

---

122 You can find the story in Jeremiah 38:1-13.

123 Louie Giglio, *Goliath Must Fall*, 242.

124 See John Robinson, *In the End, God ...*, 104-105.

each and every day is God. As in the character of God *is God.* The character of God exhibited in the goodness that is this life, that love is God. We are all free to love. We are all free to walk in the love that is God. For love is God.

Scripture can seem confusing on this matter of walking free because the Old Testament is filled with heaps of rules and regulations to live by. Most of which sound super crazy for us thousands of years later. One place in the Torah says that, guys, when you're fighting another dude, you've got to chop off his gal's hand if she tries to grab your junk.[125] Another spot suggests not wearing clothes with two different kinds of fabric woven together—so like, pretty much all modern clothing.[126] And while I could spend a few pages trying to explain why these things were normal or even good rules for this nomadic tribe of recently-freed slaves to follow, I think Jesus actually offers us a much easier hermeneutical solution—a solution that promotes living life full and free.

One of my favorite *Jesus versus religious folk* showdowns went like this: First, the temple disciples go in to question him, next, the fundamentalist Sadducees, and finally, the "progressive" Pharisees themselves, the big guns of the Judaic religious army. These were the fellas with the training, the ones with the experience, and the head-knowledge. They were known for their strict observance of the traditional Hebrew law which had them thinking they were superior to pretty much anyone and everyone—think classic narcissist. We pick up the story as they go in for the kill: "the Pharisees, hearing that he had rendered the Sadducees speechless, gathered together, and one of them

---

125 Deuteronomy 25:11-12.

126 Leviticus 19:19.

who was a lawyer, testing him, posed him the question, 'Teacher, what is the great commandment in the law?'"[127]

So, this is a scholar who has been selected for the set-up, and he has formulated this question with such perfection, that he doesn't think Jesus will have a sufficient answer. And it's a good question, a trick question, a question that actually has Jesus take the bait because Jesus replies: "You shall love the Lord your God with all your heart and with all your soul and with all your reason. This is the great and first commandment."[128] In other words, God is what's important here.

When the Pharisee and his pals hear this, they and everybody else in the crowd probably nod their heads. This was the standard answer to this question. All of the people in the crowd could have shouted out that very same answer when the Pharisee asked.[129] Then Jesus says a single word that I'm sure began to make the Pharisee sweat:

"And ... "

This is the great and first commandment *and what?* What is of equal value to the greatest? "The second is like it: You shall love your neighbor as yourself."[130]

This is classic Christianese, so let me translate to save you some time: Jesus is saying that the second is equal to the first. Second in sequence, yes, but not in significance. Meaning they go together, they are one in the same. By loving your neighbor as yourself, you are loving God because God is found in the love. This semantic distinction by Jesus is oh-so-important because in the religion Judaism had morphed into since their incredible deliverance from Egypt you

---

127 Matthew 22:34-36.

128 Matthew 22:37-38.

129 See Andy Stanley, *Irresistible*, 181.

130 Matthew 22:39.

could, on paper, love God without ever really loving those right next to you. Sadly, this is how most religions operated in the time of Jesus and, dare I say, how most continue to operate to this day. But Jesus, wanting us to walk free, follows up his already incredible statement by saying, "All of the Law and the prophets depend upon these two commandments."[131]

Jesus is literally saying, "Your entire understanding of God ought to be grounded in these two commandments. Everything you've got in your sacred texts, Genesis through Malachi, the Talmud, Mishnah, and Ketuvim are all based on these two rules to live by. It's all boiled down to love." Jesus centers his reading of scripture on the unchanging nature of God—he is saying that love is what's infallible.[132]

What would happen if we began to love on everyone as though they were God? If we began to treat everyone as though they were God? If we were to care for everybody as though there were God? What if we walked in the freedom that love provides? It can be a scary calling, to walk free. Especially when walking free means that we've left behind the comforts of normalcy. But it also serves as an opportunity. It provides us with the choice to do something with our love. To walk, wide awake, in the freedom that only love can provide. Just like Mason does and just like Ebed-melech did.

Because you have the freedom to do something constructive with your love, in love, for love, because of love.

So, go and love like it's the law—love like it's what you were made to do.

Love like it is you.

---

131 Matthew 22:40.

132 Much of the language used in this narrative from Matthew 22 first appeared in my article "Everything Over God," *Spectrum Magazine*.

17

LIGHTNING AND COUGARS AND BEARS, OH MY!

Things don't always go as planned.

I think I was about seven when my father took me backpacking for the very first time. We brought along our yellow lab, Buttercup, who sported a cute doggy backpack of her own. After a couple hundred kilometers of driving and then several more hiking, the three of us arrived at a small, wooded lake nestled somewhere in the Cascade Mountains of Washington State. I remember setting up a little orange tube tent, which my dad had received from his grandfather, on a small beach by the water's edge. After we lay our sleeping bags inside, we hung our backpacks, full of food, up in a pine tree to keep them away from local bears. The vista was truly like nothing I'd ever experienced before, untouched by the influence of man. Peaceful. Beautiful. Serene.

We went to bed early that night, well before dark, because of a storm that looked like it would roll in above us. I fell asleep quickly as my seven-year-old legs were actually pretty tired from the hike in. Only a few hours later, I awoke to my dad's relentless request that I wake up. He was shaking me, with his headlamp shining directly into my eyes and his voice filled with something I had yet to hear from my father ... fear.

"I think there is a bear outside the tent!" he half-whispered, half-yelled, as I came to.

Hearing the word "bear" was all I needed. I was out of my sleeping bag and into my jacket quicker than you can say, "Run!" Dad and I each grabbed an end of the tent and sprinted, our bare feet tripping over rocks while being pelted by the now violent storm's steady rain, nearly half-way around the lake where we eventually set it down underneath a large pine tree. Everything was soaked after our late-night marathon: the tent, our sleeping bags, and especially us!

To this day, I suspect it could have just been Buttercup who spooked us that night, but my father tells a very different version of the story. I suppose we'll never really know what happened.

Anyhow, the next morning, we stuffed all of our wet gear into our backpacks and left the lake to get back home as soon as we could. We both wanted warm showers! It helped that the sun was warm on our faces as we hiked back towards the car. Its rays danced through the pine boughs above us, creating the kind of spectacle which only nature can. As we passed through a meadow, Dad again whisper-yelled at me. (I really don't know how a "whisper-yell" is possible, but my father does a really good job at it.) There were two more bears, a mother and her cub, both snacking on berries, each on an opposite side of our trail. We put Buttercup on her leash, gave each other a high-five, and started whistling to make sure they knew we were coming.

I loved each and every moment of that trip. Bears, rain, and all.

- ♡ -

Thirteen years later, and with dozens of more backcountry experiences under my belt, a friend, Alex, and I decided to take our two dogs backpacking for the weekend. Buttercup had sadly died several years prior, but we had since procured another yellow lab, Daizy, to fill in as the resident family dog.

The four of us strolled several kilometers to a fork in the valley we had been following and set-up camp for the night. We awoke early the next morning and, after a light breakfast, set out to explore the fork to the right. I was wearing light tennis shoes with shorts and a thin cotton t-shirt, and Daizy had, well, her fur on. Our plan was to run up the valley with the dogs, looking for a lake to have all of us take a swim in. The sun was high and warm, and there wasn't a cloud in the sea-blue sky. It was a beautiful day.

We progressed up the trail and reached a vibrant meadow nestled between two wooded hillsides from where we could see what looked like a final ridgeline leading up to the massif's summit. I told Alex that Daizy and I were going to run to its top and see if we could find any lakes from the lofty perch. He and his dog opted to stay in the meadow below, chasing butterflies perhaps.

Nearly thirty minutes later, Daizy and I had made it within fifty vertical meters of the ridgeline. The sky was still clear and the sun was still shining, but Daizy wouldn't move. I called to her, begging, coaxing, demanding that she follow me. Instead, she sat, haunches in the meadow, and barked defiantly in my direction. Now I'll be honest, what she was doing was pretty dang cute. Defiant as she was, I wanted to go squeeze her little paw! But our mission of finding a lake to swim in had to take precedence! So I left defiant Daizy with her ass in the grass and kept on running up to the top of the ridge.

I couldn't have been more than a few meters from the top when I finally spotted a lake! It was small, yes, but only about a half a kilometer from where Alex and his dog were romping about in the meadow below. I began running down to the barking Daizy, overjoyed that we could finally go for a swim! As soon as I reached her, however, I knew something must be wrong because she was still barking. And Daizy isn't one to bark all that much. I looked back over my shoulder and noticed dark clouds rolling in above us. Soon after, we heard thunder. Strong winds followed.

It was time to run.

I've never seen Daizy so afraid. Her whole body was trembling. Every minute or so she went tumbling, paws over ears, down the now muddy trail. Heavy rain torrented down around us. The entire sky, which had only minutes before been a brilliant blue, was now dark and ominous. We cut across a small clearing in the trees and sprinted down towards an abandoned log cabin we had come across several hours earlier. Daizy yelped in pain as her hind leg was slowed by a prickly thicket, but she pressed on amid lightning strikes all around. Upon our arrival at the cabin, I quickly realized it wouldn't actually provide us any shelter from the rain, so we kept running. We crossed a stream and both drank as quickly as we could. I got down on all fours and went about hydrating myself just like my doggy friend. Eventually, we found a dry spot underneath a small granite boulder that was sheltered from the wind by several large trees. Huddled together for warmth, the two of us shivered under the rock as I lit a fire with some dry pine needles and the lighter stowed in my pocket.

We had become a part of the greater world around us, soaked just like the trees and trail, and I loved every moment of it.

During my sophomore year in college, time was pretty much everything.

Weekdays went something like this: four hours in class, eight hours of work, three hours of homework, an hour to eat, thirty minutes for emergency tasks (like going to the bathroom, taking a shower, etc.), maybe a half-hour for interpersonal relationships woven in between it all, and, if I was lucky, seven hours to sleep.

What made such a lifestyle worth it? Well, the easy answer is "the weekend."

A typical two-day vacation had me leaving school on Friday afternoon. I would hop into the pre-packed Gurdy and drive anywhere from two to eight hours towards some predestined destination. Upon arrival, I would promptly down several liters of water and crawl into Gurdy's trunk, pee bottle in hand, ready for a supplement-induced sleep.

I rolled over from a fetal position, looking for my frosty phone screen, and clumsily tried to mute the horrid sound of its relentlessly beeping alarm. Breakfast was downed quickly that November morning. My boots were strapped onto my feet, my backpack hoisted onto my back, and my now-full pee bottle was poured out onto a seemingly dehydrated bush next to the vacant parking lot.

It was about 7 a.m. when I finally hit the trail. I'm not sure why getting ready that particular morning had taken me so long, but, nevertheless, I was off. Three kilometers in, the trail came to a large swamp-looking area, and because of a clearing in the trees, I could finally see my intended destination: the steep north face of a 3000 meter granite peak in central Idaho.

The swampy area didn't really end but, in fact, kept on going. I spent the next four or five kilometers bushwhacking in and out amongst the trees and thickets. More than once, muddy water magically appeared in my "waterproof" Gore-Tex boots. But I kept on.

After plodding along through the swampy wasteland much longer than anticipated, I finally reached the base of the mountain. Standing below, its face looked much taller than the internet had led me to believe. To my left, I could see the popular "Sickle Couloir" ski descent, winding its way to the right. To my right, the 500 meter face I planned on soloing.

One ice screw, six nuts, two slings, four carabiners, twenty meters of six-millimeter cordelette, and a belay device were all the gear I had brought along. After about seventy meters of climbing, I was well above the point of no return. Yet, with the skies above me a bright and clear blue, I continued upwards. Hour after hour passed as I climbed higher and higher. Ice was scarce and crumbly, but after brushing aside loose powder, the rock proved solid. That being said, I never found a ledge large enough to relax on for very long. So, I wasn't able to remove my pack and take in any food or water. Without much-needed calories and hydration, I was getting more and more fatigued with each passing vertical meter. Being alone on such a large wall, without good ice or any ledges on which to rest, shook me to my core. My body was nearing its limits, my mind nearing its even more rapidly. More than once I closed my eyes and thought about how I could just lean back and all of the pain I was stupidly subjecting myself to would simply disappear. The following day, I wrote in my climbing journal that "It was the most pumped, scared, and yet focused I have been in all my life." To be honest, I don't really know about that "focused" bit, but the other two sound pretty accurate to my recollection.

Around five that evening, I finally crested the ridge. Exhausted, I collapsed in a muddled heap on the snow, my entire body shaking. I don't ever remember being so physically deteriorated in all my life. Eventually, I sat up and forced myself to take in some fluids. Once I had some water in me, my appetite grew exponentially, and I prepared myself for a feast of fruit snacks and power bars. With my body still trembling, I began digging in my rucksack for a warm cap. I had been climbing on the leeward side of the mountain, and now that I was on the ridge, the wind started to take its toll on my uncovered ears. So, I removed my helmet and placed it on my knee while exchanging it for the warm cap. As I did this, my knee, which had, at that point, been trembling for hours, shook enough to send the helmet tumbling down the opposite, oblique side of the mountain.

I remember shouting a loud "No!" as I watched the white helmet tumble down the snowy white slope. I stood up, now frantically hyperventilating, and quickly analyzed the situation. Either I could go after it, since, after all, it had cost nearly fifty dollars, or I could leave it and hike up the ridge before sundown so as to actually summit the mountain I had spent all day working so feverishly to conquer. Being as cheap as I am, I chose to forgo the summit and retrieve the darned piece of plastic.

I was in a state of anguish after descending what was at least a hundred vertical meters, while hopelessly searching for the perfectly camouflaged item. Thankfully, after twenty minutes or so, I saw it snared by a rock, just a couple dozen centimeters from an impending forty meter drop. I promptly placed it back on my head and, after hearing its strap "click," began the agonizingly long hike of following my footsteps back up to the ridgeline. By the time I returned to my backpack, darkness had fallen, and the wind had picked up drastically. I put on my headlamp, ate again, progressed down the ridge where I could glissade the steep sickle couloir I had seen from below, and then began the long, dark bushwhack back to Gurdy.

It was awful. Every stream crossing, thicket, and downed tree only worsened my already frazzled state. My heart rate was higher than I ever recall, and I was hyperventilating uncontrollably. I distinctly remember being caught in a particular thicket with the majority of my climbing rack—then attached to the outside of my backpack—being interwoven into its branches. Sweating and swearing, I frantically surged forward in an attempt to free myself, only to submerge my already soaked "waterproof" boot in another puddle of muddy water. This happened over and over again, in what seemed to be an endless fashion. Were it not for my dad's old GPS unit, I think I would have aimlessly wandered in circles. Severe vertigo coupled with a splitting headache and the deteriorating batteries in my headlamp only worsened my sense of direction.

During the flatter, meadow-like sections of the trip back, I frequently noticed animal tracks in the snow. At the time, I didn't think much of them even though most of the larger ones seemed to cross my path perpendicularly. Since being caught in that first thicket, I had been carrying a decent-sized stick, maybe six centimeters in diameter and a meter long, to help keep branches and the like out of my face. Due to my fatigued state, however, I was constantly dropping the stick and would bumble about looking for it near my feet. I was still nearly five kilometers from the car when I dropped it one final time.

I was stepping over a sizable downed tree trunk when it fell out of my hand. I remember closing my eyes, in utter fatigue, as I leaned down to retrieve it. Only several minutes prior, I had exchanged the fading batteries in my headlamp for two brand-new ones, and the light shone brightly. With my stick now in hand, I slowly straightened and opened my eyes.

It was then that I saw it.

Clear as day in the beam of my headlamp.

A cougar in mid-leap just off to my left.

I immediately swung my now wielded stick in the direction of the oncoming cat. It clearly made contact as I both felt and heard a resounding thud. At the moment, I thought I had simply imagined the mountain lion. That is, until I saw only the bottom half of the once much-longer stick in my hand and the rear-end of the cougar running off towards the trees to my left.

Unimaginably scared, I began sprinting in the direction of my car, aggravating already large blisters caused by my heavy climbing boots. Now, I know you're not supposed to run when a cougar is around. Growing up, I had read that book on US Army Ranger tactics, remember? I knew I was supposed to make myself look big! But that evening, I wasn't thinking straight. I wasn't really thinking at all.

Thankfully, I made it back to the car much faster than I assumed possible. I stripped off my sweaty layers, double-checked to be sure the doors were locked, curled up in Gurdy's trunk, and quickly fell asleep inside both of my sleeping bags. Very naked. And very afraid.

The next morning I still wasn't in my right mind. I drove well over an hour in the wrong direction before realizing my mistake. The next twenty-four hours saw me shaking almost uncontrollably. For the next month, I felt sick to my stomach every time I told the story. Even now as I write this, years later, I find myself missing the computer keys and making far more typos than usual.

Now, full disclosure: I was not in my right mind when this story took place. This wasn't like running away from bears while carrying a tent halfway around the lake during a late-night deluge. This wasn't like running through open meadows with Daizy during a big electric storm, looking for cover so as to wait it out. This experience was a whole new ball game for me. I know that there are many moments in each of our lives where we promote a figment of our imagination, spurred on perhaps by extreme circumstance, to the category of memory. For me, this could easily have been one of those instances. In all honesty, I've hesitated to tell this story at all since the further I am removed from its happening, the less I trust my own memory's recollection of events. Yet, even though I'm no longer sure there was actually a cougar who tried to attack me that night, I'm still shaken by the memory.

- ♡ -

183

Each of these three times I went into the woods, I expected something different than what actually happened to happen. When I first went backpacking with my dad, I imagined toasting marshmallows on a sandy alpine beach while watching the sun set out in the west. When I went trail running with Daizy, I expected to find a clear alpine lake for us to swim in. When I went climbing in Idaho, I expected that I would make it up to the summit and then back to the car well before nightfall. And yet, what I expected never panned out.

Similarly, when I go into a situation with the intent of showing love, something different often happens. I may go in with pure intentions, but if the environment around me shifts, or my own ego gets the better of me, my expectations are suddenly infeasible. As a pastor, I experienced this in the church setting all of the time. I would go into a sermon hoping to broaden the perspectives of my parishioners, so as to make loving *everyone* a priority. Yet, someone sitting there may have had a terrible week and could care less about my agenda of enlarging their worldview. The environment shifted. So, too, must my expectations.

Peter, a pal of Jesus, said, "Above all, have fervent love for one another, for love covers over a multitude of sins."[133] Peter is talking to a group of people here whose lives weren't quite going as they might have planned. They were oppressed.[134] Their environment had shifted from what they had foreseen to something far worse. Their intent had become obsolete, and all they wanted to do was get back to the car, get away from the bears, away from the lightning, away from the cougars, and escape. They wanted to be safe. But Peter, in his little discourse, is also providing them with an upside: love. The very DNA

---

133 1 Peter 4:8.

134 N.T. Wright & Michael Bird, *The New Testament in Its World*, 760.

of their deity. He's saying that love fixes their broken situations. That in the end, Christ, God, love, whatever you want to call the cosmic goodness, will cover the multitude of our sins, the badness we all possess, *just because.*

This means that we cannot, even with the purest of intentions, go into every situation expecting the best to come out of our fallen reality. Because we're broken—which means that things won't always be perfect—but we can have the confidence that, even in our brokenness, God sees only love. I think we too often forget how the biblical metanarrative begins not in Genesis 3, with death, dying, and decay, but in Genesis 1 where God says *everything* is good. God's calling stars good. God's calling yellow labs good. God's calling granite peaks good. God's calling humans good. God's calling *you* good. And if you don't believe me, take it from Godself who, thousands of years later, puts God in a place of vulnerability to prove it. God subjects Godself to us because God sees us as better than Godself—God let us kill God.[135] Demonstrating unbroken love in a broken world.

We've got to stop looking through the lens of our brokenness and begin seeing each other as unbroken love sees us: descendants, sons, daughters, children, offspring of the divine. Children who are of infinite value, insurmountable worth, and eternal goodness. Recognize this so that in our imperfections we aren't blindsided when our love doesn't win every battle. And instead, take courage in the fact that love will indeed win the war.[136]

Because it already has.[137]

---

135 Jesus washing feet is a great in-the-flesh example of God seeing us as better than Godself (Matthew 26:14-39; Luke 22:24-27; John 13:1-17).

136 See Rob Bell, *Love Wins*, 119.

137 John 16:33.

18

"WHAT'S GOING ON, GUYS?"

After proposing on top of a mountain and asking forgiveness for not driving her back from getting that kid-stopper, it was finally time for Jo and I to get our partnership federally recognized (you know, because love ... and tax breaks).

We had both been working lots of extra shifts at a combined nine jobs for a combined 150 hours a week to pay for all of the planning we were doing (well, mostly to pay for school). We were going to get married in a barn, my friend Paddy was going to roast us at the ceremony, and my cousin was all lined-up to take the pictures. We had even gone so far as to make a catering reservation at our favorite food spot, Taqueria Yungapeti.[138] Everything was set for our June wedding date.

Several months before the wedding was to take place, I moved down to Arizona for my first big-boy job out of college where, in the first week, I was called "satanic" for "hypnotizing" my parishioners. So yeah. Jo had one more quarter of school to finish up, so she stayed in Washington but came to visit me once, which was really nice. We also texted and did video chats, so it wasn't like a real long-distance

---

138 I would move back to my college town, if for nothing else, just to live near this restaurant. It is that good. 7 of 5 stars.

relationship back in the 1700s where you could only communicate via fancy letters and messenger pigeons.

The evening before I left for Arizona everyone convened at Tommy and Joel's apartment where I had been showering and regularly doing laundry since moving into Ken. Tyler, Tommy, Joel, Jo, and I were all gathered around Chad and his guitar while he serenaded us. So many of my favorite people shared stories, laughs, and songs for hours into the night. That may be the most bittersweet memory I have; I'll carry it with me always. The next morning they all came out again as I prepared to drive away in Ken. Some handed me notes. Some gave kisses. All shared their love. I cried for the first thirty minutes of driving—with sixteen hours to go after that. My heart was so heavy thinking about how much my life was changing. I was grateful for the memories but so saddened to leave the familiarity of my dearest friends.

Three months later, I flew back to Washington a week before our wedding. Let me tell you, there was a lot to do. One day we were hunting for wild lavender, and the next we ended up being the local taxi service. We never really knew what was coming our way!

Two days before the big event, things really came to a head. It was a Tuesday, which already isn't particularly my favorite day of the week. I was still blue from the Boston Bruins' Stanley Cup Final loss in game seven less than a week before, and things kept growing worse and worse as the hours leading up to the wedding ticked down. Two days prior, on Sunday, Jo was supposed to have moved out of her apartment. But, being that her apartment was the only place near the barn with enough space to store all of our wedding decorations, she turned in her key but used the pin pad on the backdoor to gain entry. On top of that, Jo's aunt had graciously ordered flowers for the occasion and shipped them to her theoretically vacant apartment. Which again, she wasn't supposed to be able to gain entry to. The flowers had been scheduled to come sometime that Tuesday morning but hadn't arrived yet. In addition, everyone else was so caught up in their particular areas of planning that Jo and I were the only ones left to go pick up a bridesmaid from an airport over four hours away. (As you can imagine, there had been a lot of miscommunication that day, too.) So, we loaded our little blue Toyota with a bunch of rejected wedding fundamentals that we planned to drop off at my folks' on our way to the airport, and were off. Needless to say, the two of us were starting to get pretty stressed-out.

The backseat was filled with the rejected items all collected in several large black trash bags. I was driving and Jo had the radio turned up quite loudly so as to drown out our woes. The sun was high and hot, and I had my shirt off exposing the upper half of my body which was in desperate need of a tan for the wedding. Half-way to my parent's, Jo's phone rang. It was Joel. At our request, he had kindly gone to her old apartment to spend the afternoon inside waiting for the flowers to arrive. Jo turned the radio down and put him on speaker.

"Hey, so I can't get in your apartment," he said, "What's the code again?"

Jo gave it to him, and we waited for him to make another attempt.

"Yeah, that's what I thought. It doesn't work."

And with that, Jo started to freak out, "Niq, what if they changed the code? We won't be able to get the stuff out for the wedding!"

I kept looking over at Jo, trying to console her, but it wasn't really working. Joel did his best to be sympathetic and said he would just wait for the flowers outside in the driveway.

Both of our hearts started to race. As my heart picked up speed, so did the car.

Moments later we passed a police car parked on the opposite side of the highway. In an instant, the red and blue lights affixed atop its roof were ablaze. I pulled over, rolled down my window, put my keys on the dash, and placed my hands on the wheel. Jo hung up the phone, and we waited.

By the time the officer had reached my window, Jo was sobbing uncontrollably. But the words that came out of the officer's mouth came softly, "What's going on, guys?" Not, "Why were you speeding?" Not, "It seems like you all are crazy people with trash in your backseat, all this crying, and no shirt!" Not, "Do you know how fast you were going, son?"

"What's going on, guys?"

I did my best to explain: "We're getting married, and somehow we ended up as everyone's taxi cab, and I have to drop this stuff off at my folks' place, and we think we're locked out of her apartment where all of the decorations are, but it's really our fault; we should have just extended her lease by an extra week, and I'm sorry I was speeding, but she was crying a lot, and I was just freaked out at the situation!" He smiled and asked if I knew how fast I was going. I knew I was going fast, again, when my heart rate speeds up so does the car, but I wasn't sure just how fast. He knew, though. As it turns out, I was going twenty-five kilometers per-hour over the speed limit.

Now, to some of you that may not seem very fast at all. But I am very conservative when it comes to driving. It's like me and airports, I always want a buffer: go five kilometers an hour under and get to the terminal five hours before departure. It's just my rule of thumb. And it's not like I'd never been pulled over before. In fact, I'd been pulled over lots of times. Mostly for dumb little things like a license plate light, or a taillight, or a brake light (and then lots more times for living out of my car and petting cats), but never for speeding. These were uncharted waters.

The officer went back to his squad car with my paperwork, and I looked over at Jo and said, "Man, I must look like some kind of wife-beater with all of this trash in the back and no shirt and you crying."

She smiled at me, and we started laughing at our rib-tickling situation. Yet, even with our moment of joy amidst the turmoil, I was really worried about the fine to come.

He wasn't gone long, so as he walked back I thought, *This could come out to several hundred dollars. I sure hope we get that much money in wedding gifts.*

"Enjoy your wedding," he said smiling as he handed me back my license, registration, and insurance, "I wish you two the best."

We were floored. We didn't expect that kind of grace. We didn't dare hope for that kind of forgiveness. We didn't deserve that kind of love. *But we were given it anyway.*

This is the beauty of the body of love.

Alone, I cannot do what that officer did. As much as I'd love to, I cannot forgive speeding tickets; I don't have the authority. Alone, I'm a single contributor. But it is when we all join together that we begin to bear the burden of each other's shortcomings. Paul says that *"all* have sinned."[139] You are not exempt! And neither am I! *All* are imperfect. *All* have problems. *All* suck.

But we, as the body of love, can work to change that. Brené Brown quotes her pastor as saying, "In order for forgiveness to happen, something has to die. If you make a choice to forgive, you have to face into the pain. You simply have to hurt."[140] Forgiveness hurts! It takes from us what we feel we are entitled to, what we know deep down we deserve. One of my undergraduate professor's children was murdered

---

139 Romans 3:23. Emphasis added.

140 Brené Brown, *Rising Strong*, 150.

in cold blood. While he indeed experienced incredible hurt, pain, and turmoil through the process of forgiving his daughter's perpetrator, he somehow forgave nonetheless.[141]

There is this really strange string of stories in the Hebrew Bible that demonstrate a similar kind of forgiveness. It's found in the relationship between two people who actually had a lot in common: Saul and David. We can assume they were both of the same cultural and racial background: They were both men, neither were of royal blood prior to their coronation, and both were leading a people eager to have a flesh-and-blood king at the helm, which God didn't appear to be all that happy about since God compares it to idol-worship![142] And Saul, who was somewhat of a narcissist, seemed to really hate David for his military successes, even trying to kill him on multiple occasions![143] But what did David do? David, the sinner, the guy who was by no means perfect?[144] He *loved* Saul. When Saul ends up dying, not at David's hand but by other means, he weeps.[145] David figured out a way to love and forgive the man who *hated* him. Human logic cannot fathom such forgiveness—our heads just can't comprehend

---

141 For more on this incredible story pick up a copy of Darold Bigger's book, *A Time to Forgive.*

142 See 1 Samuel 8:7-8.

143 E.g. 1 Samuel 18:10-11; 2 Samuel 1:11-16.

144 David murdered a guy after raping his wife (2 Samuel 11) and he supposedly killed tens of thousands of others on the battlefield (1 Samuel 29:5); David was not perfect, or even close to it, no matter how much Christians may laude him. So maybe enough with teaching kids about his vicious encounter with a giant? Please? Oh and the flood is a terrible children's story too—God committing genocide is exactly what we need our young people reading about without any kind of textual criticism. Need I go on? Just stop it!

145 2 Samuel 1:11-12.

such selfless and, at times, sacrificial love.[146] To our pea-sized brains, goodness like that simply doesn't make sense.

Yet, we can choose to live our lives in the unknown. We can be intentional about living our lives with a heart of forgiveness, just like David, just like my professor, and just like Jo's and my officer friend, because forgiveness is the very heart of love.

Forgiveness is the very nature of love.

Because our forgiveness *is* only love.

Our whole pre-wedding fiasco ended up being pretty pointless.

Jo's bridesmaid got a bus ticket for the next morning and spent the night with a friend who lived near the airport. The code to Jo's apartment hadn't been changed; Joel just didn't know that he also needed to turn the deadbolt to get inside. And two days later, on a drizzly turned sunny Thursday, people from all of the wide-reaching facets of our lives came together as one. Different, yes. Variant, of course. But all wrapped up into one big, smiling family.

That's only love, too.

---

146 See N.T. Wright, *Surprised by Hope*, 101.

19

THE MOUNTIE

As image-bearers of the divine love, we have the privilege of forgiving, of cutting those around us some slack, of loving *all* no matter what. Yet sometimes, during the long dark winter months, I need to be reminded of such privilege more regularly.

I had been sitting alone in my college dorm room staring at my computer screen day after day, weekend after weekend, week after week, and it had me gloomy. The weather everywhere was terrible. For some odd twenty-year-old reason, sitting around just wasn't cutting it for me. It had been days since I had set foot outside, weeks since I had seen the sun, and months since I had been in the alpine I so desperately craved.

It was mid-February in the Pacific Northwest, smack in the middle of an oddly harsh winter. So, when a coveted long-weekend came around, there were to be no excuses for the weather being bad. No matter the cold, no matter the clouds, no matter the snow, I was going north—to Canada.

Late one Friday afternoon, we packed my friend Tyler's little red Honda sedan full of winter climbing and camping gear. Then we stuffed in four full-sized humans, along with one outrageously over-sized drone, and began our long drive up to the great white north.

Thankfully, Chad, who needed a ride to the airport "only forty-five minutes into the trip" and "couldn't find a ride with anyone else," only needed a ride forty-five minutes into the trip. Soon we were rid of him and the very large carry-on item he had been forced to straddle in the back seat. This left only Joel, Tyler, and myself in the little red car spinning its way north.

Kilometer after kilometer of asphalt sped underneath us while Joel's favorite podcast episodes blended seamlessly with Tyler's playlist of Latin pop hits. Tired as I may have been after a week filled with paper-writing and late-night shifts at work, Joel and Tyler's near-constant bantering, stops at just about every Tim Horton's we passed, along with the intermittent deep conversation or two, was more than enough to keep me from catching a wink of sleep during the twelve-hour drive. According to Google Maps, it could have taken quite a lot longer, but Tyler is an expert at "putting the pedal to the metal," as it were.

Eventually, sometime around 5 a.m., we arrived at the gloriously snow-covered paradise that is the Rocky Mountains of western Alberta. We promptly found ourselves an abandoned parking lot just off the main highway to call home for the remainder of the night. I slept like a purring kitty, rolling over onto Joel only a time or two in the four hours Tyler had allotted for our sleep.

Most mornings I wake up to the pre-programmed "beep-beep-beep" of my cell phone. However, this particular morning I was awakened by a significantly more disturbing sound—a steady stream of yellow liquid torrenting down the outside of my single-walled tent.

Rain it was not. Tyler's dehydrated urine it was.[147]

After his disgusting deluge had ceased, I started swinging blind punches in the general direction of what I sleepily thought was Tyler, so as to teach the young man a lesson. This resulted in an aggressive

---

147 Tyler claims the "urine" was just a trickle of water from his bottle intended to make Joel and myself believe it was a bodily fluid. I still think it was pee, so I guess he won this particular round of wits.

tussle with my now wide-awake tentmate, Joel, which escalated even further when Tyler thought it would be funny to remove a few of the supporting poles from our tent.

Eventually, after sorting out our differences, we packed up the little red sedan and drove to our trip's first ice climbing destination.

We had a fun day at the crag. Two of us tried our hand at climbing various routes of local waterfall ice. Joel, being brand new to ice climbing, decided it best to toprope a pitch for starters. Then, after a less than desirable first experience, he proceeded to not climb any more that day. A peculiar decision indeed, since this was an ice climbing trip. Instead, the day found Joel sitting, standing, and filming Tyler and myself climb on his obnoxiously large flying camera.

That evening, as the temperatures began to drop lower and lower, our minds started to wander to warmer places: Tahiti, Belize, Dante's Inferno. Eventually, our daydreaming turned to more realistic aspirations, like three sleeping bags and one particularly unsanitary tent. After hiking back to the car, we started driving, looking for another abandoned parking lot for the night. Inching the Honda up a snow-covered side road, we sleepily passed a sign that looked like one of those no-smoking signs you see outside of supermarkets. This one just had the cigarette replaced by a teepee. While it worried us at first, we eventually breathed a collective sigh of relief and assured one another that none of us had brought a teepee along.

After parking, Joel and I proceed to set up the now frozen pee-tent, or was it tent-pee? Maybe we did have a *t-pee* after all! Anyway, as the two of us fumbled about in the dark trying to insert tent poles into the places tent poles go, Tyler once again cleared room for himself in the backseat of his Honda. Truth be told, we were working fairly proficiently when compared to the prior night's 5 a.m. camp set-up antics. We even took to complementing one another regarding our obviously improved work ethic and organizational skills!

Once camp was set-up, we ate heartily, stretched out our tired legs and forearms, and then sat down in the backseat of Tyler's rig to review some of the day's footage Joel had captured with his drone. Take my word for it, because I doubt Joel will ever release any of the footage online, but the videos were actually pretty cool. Tyler and I realized that maybe the footage we were viewing on Joel's computer could actually make us famous. That's how good it was: *famous footage!* Right then and there, huddled in the backseat of Tyler's tiny sedan, we asked Joel for forgiveness regarding all of the emotional trauma we had put him through because of his solitary toprope climb. It was a most joyous and vulnerable moment for all three of us. We were bonding hardcore!

The raw and fluid emotion of true brotherhood we had experienced leading up to this moment was quickly popped, as if a bubble, when red and blue colors suddenly flashed into view behind us. Blinding headlights followed. Unmistakably, this was the famous mounted police force of Canada, and they were here to take away Joel's contraband. You see, earlier in the day, Joel had been informed by a local that he might be filming in part of a national park's no-fly zone, after which he stopped. However, since he hadn't deleted the footage, he quickly hid his computer under Tyler's pillow so as to avoid arrest— Joel has never been too keen on getting arrested.

The three of us got out of the backseat and calmly walked towards the squad car where the officer was waiting. We were honestly quite surprised not to see the Mountie riding in on a moose, but the car was cool, too, I guess. The officer asked us if we had been drinking. In unison we shouted, "Water!" Looking confused, he proceeded to check the car's plates. Doing this really made us feel like foreigners. It's worth mentioning that both Tyler and his car had come all the way from the great state of Colorado, and Colorado is pretty darn far from Alberta!

As the Mountie retreated back to his trusty steed so as to check on the plate's validity, I just about opened my mouth to say, "Sir, we don't even have a teepee! And you can't arrest us foreigners like this when we didn't break any rules! We have added so much money into your economy! I mean, you have no idea how much my friend, Tyler, has already invested at Tim Horton's, and we haven't even been in Canada for twenty-four hours!"

Thankfully, I kept the old rat trap shut. Instead of getting arrested in a foreign country, the automobile-Mountie simply told us to pack up and be out of the parking lot before all of the hotel sleepers showed up the next morning to go snow hiking. That moose-wrangler was actually a pretty nice guy! Way nicer than he ever needed to be.

Now I'll be the first to admit that I have broken rules. Yes, sometimes even intentionally. And when I'm confronted by authority, fearing that I'm going to get in trouble, I often lie, I freeze up, I try to cover my tracks because I want to be seen as perfect. The problem? I'm not.

I was scrolling through Twitter the other day and came across this quote from Bob Goff that says, "Grace draws a circle around everyone and says we're in."[148] Let that sink in for a second: *You are in.* Your lack of perfection is not a deterrent to a God of only love. In fact, as C.S. Lewis wrote, "Look for Christ and you will find Him, and with Him everything else thrown in."[149] That inclusivity, that "inness," is the

---

148 I later found the line in one of Goff's books, *Live in Grace, Walk in Love*, 95.

149 C.S. Lewis, *Mere Christianity*, 227.

result of only love. A kind of love that still lets us camp out in a snowy parking lot even after we blatantly disobey the signage.

If you grew up reading the Bible, you might have missed out on the message of "inness" as demonstrated throughout the ancient text. But when we look closely we see, even in the Old Testament, a God of long-term radical inclusivity. It is this oft forgotten theme throughout the Hebrew Bible which keys us into a reality that, in the end, everyone takes part in a loving relationship with God.[150] The first place this promise appears is in God's covenant with Abraham where we're told that all nations on earth will be blessed through his family line.[151] I grew up thinking that "all nations" meant like one or two lucky chaps from each country. So maybe Ghandi and Mother Teresa from India, Martin Luther King Jr and my mom from the United States, and so on. But God's blessing for all nations is actually *for all nations*. As in all peoples. Everywhere. No matter their cultural heritage or socioeconomic status. Every individual is a recipient of God's promised blessing. Ancient Near Eastern cultures were collectivist, not individualistic like ours, so when you spoke of a nation, you were really talking about every person that nation represented—as in *everyone.*[152] That is the kind of inclusive God the Bible demonstrates, where in the end there is:

> A great crowd that no one was able to number, from every nation, and from tribes and peoples and tongues, standing before the throne and before the suckling lamb, clad in white robes, and date palms in their

---

150 An Old Testament foreshadowing of this can be seen in Psalm 86:9.

151 Genesis 12:2, 18:18.

152 E. Richards & Richard James, *Misreading Scripture with Individualistic Eyes*, ix.

hands, and they cry out in a loud voice, saying, "Salvation to our God who sits upon the throne, and to the suckling lamb."[153]

Perhaps this sounds way too good to be true (unless you hate white robes and palm branches, which could very easily be the case): every individual receives the blessing of God through the family of Abraham. But as Paul says, looking through the contextual lens of the Old Testament, "just as by one transgression unto condemnation for all human beings, *so also by one act of righteousness unto rectification of life for all human beings.*"[154] Only love means that, no matter who you are, no matter what you've done, no matter how much you suck, *you're in.* The goodness of God will restore all of our corrupt creation, even the worst of the worst![155] So, no matter who you are, no matter what you've done, love has got you. Grace has drawn a circle around us all and set us free. And because of that gift, you and I have the opportunity to share that grace with those around us.

We have the chance to cut people some slack for the sake of love—because I don't want my invitation list to the kingdom of infinite love to be shorter than love's guest slate.

The day after our encounter with the gracious Mountie, we climbed at a couple of new waterfalls and, once again, Joel toproped a solitary pitch, after which he just sat around (as he didn't want to risk flying his drone anymore). We made sure not to give him any

---

153 Revelation 7:9-10.

154 Romans 5:18. Emphasis added.

155 Origen has a great systematic dialogue on this subject in, *On First Principles*, 70.

crap this time because of the footage he did have—we just knew it was going to make us famous! Of course, we went to Tim Horton's a few more times, then made a big meal in a nicely-heated public washroom. After dinner we took much-needed "baths" in several trough-style bathroom sinks. We again drove to the no teepee spot where we had met our Mountie friend the night before, hoping to run into him again. Maybe he would ride-in on a moose this time! Sadly, neither he nor his fuzzy companion ever showed up.

On the road towards home the next morning, we exchanged fond memories of our trip, talked about relationships and the like, shared stories from our childhoods, as well as listened to plenty more podcasts and Latin pop hits. We even stopped off at a hot spring to relax and take real baths. It was a wonderful day.

As night fell, it began snowing a little. Joel was driving, and Tyler and I had worked to rearrange our cramped spaces in the maxed-out car so as to try and catch some shut eye. Then, just before I shut my eyes, I witnessed one of the strangest phenomena I have ever observed.

Time slowed down.

Joel had taken an icy right turn far too fast and spun the car to the left in the direction of an oncoming truck. As the vehicle came speeding towards Tyler's little red Honda, I realized our spin pattern would line the right side of our car perfectly with its front end. Since I was riding shotgun, it just so happens that the right side of my body was what the big truck would most certainly make first contact with. So, I scooted left just a tad.

Upon impact—with the adjacent snowbank—we collectively breathed a sigh of relief, and I scooted back over to the right. Thankfully, the driver of the truck was wide-awake at the time and had swerved to his left as we slid across the road to his right. Missing us and the right side of my body by mere centimeters.

We were pretty well stuck in the snowbank, but it was no big deal since the truck's driver helped to pull us out with his enormous rig. He was a seriously nice guy. Almost as nice as that moose-wrangling Mountie.

Tyler then took over as the driver, and the two of us vowed to never let Cali-boy-Joel drive again—anywhere—regardless of the weather. We crossed the border around midnight and were greeted by a cheery border officer who made fun of Joel being a business major by saying, "Hey, I went to business school, too, and look where it got me!" Joel sleepily muttered something about government benefits as Tyler accelerated the little red Honda towards home. Speeding, of course, so that we could arrive back to school just in time for morning classes.

20

STRANGE SAVIORS

"These f***ing bees, man!" was the first thing my ears heard only moments after my bare feet hit the already sweltering pavement, "These bees have been after me all night!"

I had spent the past few hours sleeping in my car, parked alongside the interstate because, less than a week before in sunny southern California, my grandmother was involved in an automobile accident. She was about to take a left-hand turn on her way to the store to get the weekend's groceries, checked for oncoming traffic, and proceeded forward. No more than a few seconds later another vehicle hit her Honda Odyssey broadside. She said a tree in between the lanes must have impeded her vision. The van was totaled. Her ribs were cracked, there were bruises all along her chest where the seat belt caught her. Her hand and fingers sported burns from the airbags as they opened all around her. She was shaken and rushed to the hospital. But she was alive. Her van had saved her.

At the time, I lived only seven hours from my grandma's house and so a few days after the accident, I went to visit her after work.

I arrived after midnight, and then curled up to sleep in the backseat of my sedan so as not to wake everyone inside by my arrival. Only two days later, I was on my way home as I had to get back for work. Again, I left in the evening. As midnight approached, I was still over 200 kilometers from home. I pulled over at a truck stop along the interstate, once again curled up in the backseat of my car, and went to sleep.

Sleeping in cars is not new to me. As a kid, I always found a way to conform to the coziest of backseat positions on long road trips. When I got my first car, Gurdy, the summer before my senior year in high school, it wasn't long before the backseat was exchanged for a mattress extending into the trunk. I loved it. I could sleep anywhere.

A few years later, in my junior year of college, I traded out that first car for the cargo van you know as Ken. After only a few weeks, the tool chests and rubber floor mats from the previous owner who ran a tire company had been replaced by a bed frame and mattress. Again, I could sleep anywhere. Again, I loved it. I slept in that van almost every night through to the end of college, and it saved me thousands of dollars on rent.

- ♡ -

I woke up around 6:30 a.m. at the interstate truck stop. Groggy, stinky, and sweaty from a night sealed-up in the car. My hair was amuck. My eyes were still half-shut. Uncurling from the fetal position, I opened-up the rear door and stepped outside into the already eighty-degree Nevada air.

Then, as my feet hit the pavement, I heard it: "These f***ing bees, man! These bees have been after me all night!"

To my left, three parking spots over, stood a man. Thick Jersey accent, bright red T-shirt, somewhere in his mid-sixties, standing next to a dilapidated, black Mercedes. He immediately began to walk in my direction, leaned his large body up against the trunk of my navy blue 'yota, and motioned to a bee, struggling to get through my rear window. "He's after you, too, the mother f***er! Must be the same little sh*t who was after me all night!"

The man's name was Mitch. As we were exchanging names, I went in for the traditional handshake, but all he wanted was a firm pre-Covid fist-bump. As soon as I told him my name was Niq, he started calling me "Niqi."

I liked Mitch.

We talked for several minutes about bees, where I was headed, where he was going, his upbringing in New York City, my grandmother whom I had just visited, and, eventually, his mother. He proceeded to tell me about how he had moved his mother from New York to Florida, how their house was flooded during Hurricane Ima, how they lost everything because they didn't have flood insurance when the storm hit, and how his mother had died shortly after they evacuated the state: "We lost everything; I lost everything," he said.

Eventually, our conversation shifted to cars, our two cars, specifically. "I got Betty," that was his black Mercedes, "for 1500 dollars when I moved out here after I left Florida. I had to get outta there. Nothing good there anymore! You can't do anything, it's all lost."

His face had fallen. And remember, I liked Mitch. I don't usually like all that many people in the first ten minutes of talking. Especially when they're telling me a sob story. But for some reason, I got him. Here's a man who could easily be my granddad, living out of his car, hopping around from truck stop to truck stop trying to avoid the security detail who think of him as a pest. (A security guard had pulled up several minutes before and asked me, *me*, the groggy, stinky, sweaty child with his hair amuck and eyes still half-shut, who had also just spent the night sleeping in his car, if I was okay! All because Mitch was leaning into my old Toyota—a car with the paint chipping up on the roof and a large dent in the rear driver's side door from a previous owner.) After the security officer pulled away, Mitch looked me in the eye and asked intensely, "How old are you, Niqi?"

"Twenty-three," I replied.

"Get your life together before you're thirty, kid," he said. "That means you've got, what, five, six years?"

A tear began to roll down his cheek. I could tell he wanted to say more, but emotion had overcome him. I went in for the hug, and he gladly reciprocated.

Holding back more tears he asked, "Do you got an education, a girl?"

"Yes," I said as I began to fight back tears of my own, "Yes, I'm lucky, sir; I've got both."

"Well you hang on to those," he replied. "You hang on to those and never let go."

We embraced for another ten to fifteen seconds in silence—not an awkward silence, *meaningful silence*. Two strangers, who just so happened to sleep in the same parking lot, at the same truck stop, along the same interstate, in the same state, who smelled equally as bad as the other, who looked equally as bad as one another, hugged it out as though we had known each other for years.

As we both stepped back, he asked, sincerely, "Do you have enough gas to get where you're going?"

"I think I'll make it alright," I replied, again about to cry. This homeless man was offering me, someone with a steady income, a roof over my head, and a running car, what might have equated to his meals for the week. Saying that I was taken aback by his generosity would be an understatement.

Mitch began walking towards Betty, then glanced back over his shoulder at me while he pointed at her, and said, tenderly, "Without her, I'd be dead. Without her," he motioned with his thumb as though he were choking himself with an invisible piece of string, "I'd be like a noose around my neck. I'd be f***ing dead."

His car had saved him. But little did he know, Mitch, in his incomprehensible generosity, had saved me.[156]

That's exactly what our love, our generosity, does. Love saves.[157]

Love provides a way out for *everyone*. Rich and poor. Homeless and home-bound. Abled and disabled. Love isn't this exclusive club where the "holy" or the "perfect" get to hang out. Let me say it a bit more bluntly: love is not a building with a steeple and a cross on top.

As modern Christians, we've made our churches into the temple that God never even asked for.[158] In the ancient Near East, people worshiped image-gods, statues made of wood, stone, or metal. They would house their statues in their temples—temples almost identical to the temple Solomon built for the Hebrew's God. But long before that temple was built, God moved around in a tent, the tabernacle, which God seemed to like a lot. Things changed, however, when the Israelites decided that, just as when they wanted a king, they wanted a physical structure to house their God, too. It is here that we see God stooping to the role we humans would have God play—building the temple and God's habitation of it were but concessions, accommodations with the goal of gaining relationship with the people over time. For once the temple was built and God moved in, the people,

---

156 This story first appeared in audio format as "Strangers as Saviors," *The Young Project Podcast.*

157 1 John 4:10.

158 The temple was clearly David's idea, not God's; God goes so far as to disapprove of David's desire to build it in 1 Chronicles 17:4.

Solomon included, began to see God as somewhat domesticated. God was suddenly defined spatially, by geography. Once God was moved into God's own temple, God was reduced to the level of any other pagan deity who, too, lived in a temple.[159] Gone were the days of a moving tent; eventually, gone too was God's spirit from the building intended to house God because God didn't, and still doesn't, need some building to make a difference. "Church" as we understand it in the religious sense was never in the cards for God.

What God really does is pronounce sinners to be holy. And God sure as heck doesn't need some building you go to once a week to do that. The love of this mobile, omnipresent God says, "What little I have *is for you*." Through such inclusivity, the love that is God provides a way for us all to become increasingly conscientious of the greater body of which we all are a part and conscientious, too, of the Spirit which inhabits our collective temple.[160] As Pierre Teilhad de Chardin says, "God does not offer Himself to our finite beings as things all complete and ready to be embraced. For us, He is eternal discovery and eternal growth. The more we think we understand Him, the more he reveals himself as otherwise."[161] In other words, love gives us the liberty to move beyond ourselves, or our "sacred" places, and progress into an infinitely bigger, broader, deeper understanding of how incomprehensible love really is.

Because love is as incomprehensible as a homeless man offering to pay for someone's gas.

Love saves. That is what it does.

And because we're love, we can too.

---

159 Andy Stanley, *Irresistible*, 45.

160 See 1 Corinthians 6:19-20.

161 Pierre Teilhard de Chardin, *Divine Milieu*, 139.

21

A FEW HEAVY BAGS

I love Boston; it's a part of my history—the old self which informs my new. The USS Constitution. Fenway Park. The Public Gardens. Duck boats. The Bruins. Harvard. The Freedom Trail. It's such a nostalgic place to visit and a terribly difficult place to leave.

On one particular trip, I spent several days in town, visiting both family and my favorite hockey team. After the fun was over, it came time for me to fly back to Portland, Oregon, where my car was parked, and then drive back to school. On my way to Boston, I had a layover in Minneapolis, and coming back, I had a layover as well. So, when my uncle dropped me off at the airport that evening, I printed off my ticket at the kiosk, went through security, grabbed a bagel at Dunkin', and found the gate for my flight to Minneapolis.

Now, I like to be early for things like plane rides. Anytime you spend money on something that can, quite literally, fly away without you, I really don't like to risk it. I've actually been known to get to the airport ten hours before a flight left (more on that in a few paragraphs)! And this flight to Minneapolis was no different. I sat there at the gate for almost two hours waiting for my flight to board, reading a book, writing a term paper, listening to music. You know, normal airport stuff.

It was almost time to board when, over the terminal loudspeakers, I heard something I thought I'd never hear in all of my life: "Passenger

Niqolas Ruud, please come to gate C17 service to Denver. Niqolas Ruud to gate C17, your flight is about to depart."

I was like, *Wait, what? Denver? C17? I'm supposed to be waiting for a flight to Minneapolis! This whole time I've just been chilling at A5? This can't be right.* I looked at my ticket. There it was in black and white: "Denver, C17." I had been so caught up in my past, thinking I was having a layover in Minneapolis again, that I forgot to look for where I was really going.

So, I got up and started running. I had a small suitcase and a backpack and was running as fast as I could with them in tow. I must have been in some kind of a basement level because I could have sworn I ran up four or five flights of stairs. I ran to the end of Terminal A, past Terminal B, and into Terminal C. I was tired, discouraged, and hungry for more than the one bagel I had consumed two hours before. Then, in my despair, I saw something life-giving in the distance: a flat escalator! It was like a river of hope in a desert wasteland!

There is something, however, that sometimes makes me wish I were just running alongside moving walkways: people on the conveyor who refuse to move. I'm like, *Why are you standing there?! Why are you standing on this flat escalator? You could stand anywhere else in the airport, and I wouldn't be mad!* I was half-way down the moving walkway, I could see gate C17 in the distance, but I was stuck. A beautiful family of five, with two strollers and a massive suitcase that should have been checked, was blocking my path.

Something that was supposed to expedite my journey ended up slowing me down instead.

- ♡ -

Several years later, during my last summer of freedom before graduating college, I took an internship out at a church in the humid flatlands of middle-America. This part of the world is affectionately referred to by those who have never lived anywhere else as, "America's Heartland." Others call it the "Midwest," although I'm not sure how it classifies as "mid" or "west" when looking at the continental United States in its present form.

Now, as you may have already deciphered from the rest of this book, the vast majority of my post-adolescent life up to this point had been spent living in areas where mountains were nearby and big city life seemed far, far away. Dayton, Ohio, however, was (and I'm sure still is) a really big city. When I flew out towards Dayton that fateful summer day, with only my bike, two backpacks, and a big yellow duffel bag in tow, I wasn't prepared for how hard it would be for this country boy to actually get moved into the big city.

Traveling on the church's dollar, I decided to go mega-cheap and purchased the plane tickets from an airline I will henceforth call "Front-Tear" (aptly named for all of the crying they inflict on their many passengers). Jo, the sweetest of sweethearts, had graciously dropped me, my bike, my backpacks, and my big yellow duffel bag off at the Boise airport in southwestern Idaho. She left me there several hours early so that she could get back to a visiting friend, and, as you might presume from such a tear-inflicting airline, as soon as she had left, my flight was promptly delayed. In the end, I spent a combined *ten hours* waiting there in the airport for the plane to get itself ready to go.

After takeoff, we flew about an hour and a half southeast to Denver, Colorado, arriving at around two in the morning. Knowing that my next flight had also been delayed and wasn't scheduled to leave until eight, I found a secluded corner above the food courts, blew up my lightweight climbing mattress which had been conveniently tucked into my carry on, and fell into a shallow sleep.

Waking the next morning, I drowsily made my way to a flight screen and found that, again, my flight which had been scheduled to leave at eight, had also been delayed several hours. After catching a few more winks and drafting the introduction to this book (inspiration strikes in the strangest of places), I made my way to the gate, only to find that this time my flight had been canceled in full.

Drowsy from the uncomfortable and noisy night of sleep, I tipsily made my way to the Front-Tear service counter with the intent of rescheduling. After nearly an hour of standing in line, I struggled to keep my cool when the agent behind the booth told me that I could hop on a flight on its way to Cleveland *only* eight hours in the future. Yes, Cleveland, as in the city, not the basketball team, and not Columbus, the city where I should have arrived more than a dozen hours prior. After some poor negotiating on my end, I left the airline's service counter with a new ticket for a flight to Cincinnati sixteen hours in the future, and no food or hotel voucher to redeem during the duration of my time in Denver.

Sixteen hours isn't all that much in retrospect of my entire life; that being said, it sure did seem like a long time while it was going on. To make matters worse, the airline wouldn't automatically transfer my checked items, the 150-liter duffel bag and shrink-wrapped road bike, to my new flight departing the next day. So, I had to leave the airport's terminal area with all of the bathrooms and restaurants and make my way down to baggage claim so as to un-check my checked luggage. Then, all I had to do was sit on a bench next to the baggage claim carousel listening to the classic, "Attention all passengers. For your safety, do not leave any personal items unattended … Report all unneeded items to the nearest TSA representative," over the loudspeaker for the next sixteen sleepless hours.

Combined, my bike and three bags were pretty heavy. As such, I couldn't just get up and go to the bathroom down the hall or run to the central food court to grab a bite to eat without risking a TSA representative noticing that I had left them behind. What if they thought I was an eco-friendly cycling terrorist or something? That could have been terrible! So, to avoid getting arrested, I did my best to just sit there and limit any physical exertion which might burn precious calories. I didn't have any food, nor had I eaten since Jo dropped me off in Boise almost twenty-four hours prior. I knew that if I rationed the small amount of water I had in my bottle, I could at least last until the Front-Tear ticketing gate opened up at 3:30 a.m., fourteen hours in the future.

And so, at twelve noon, I took out a book and began to read. I read for a few hours, finished the book, and took out another. A few hours later, I was finished with the second one as well, and took out a third. Believe it or not, I read three books before the sun set that evening and then worked to write this very chapter! Needless to say, no matter how nourished my mind may have been, my stomach was none the wiser. At one point, I hid all of my stuff behind a big billboard outside of the baggage claim and snuck out from behind it carrying nothing but my phone and wallet. Seconds after stepping away from my new lair, I made eye-contact with a TSA representative and promptly turned back around, head hung in shame.

I was nearing starvation. Well, not really. I was nearing boredom. And I was getting pretty dehydrated.

So I made a Tinder account.

One of the books I had read that afternoon mentioned something about how millennials don't just use apps like Tinder to get a date, but some also use it to make friends or meet people with similar interests.[162] And while, according to some, I'm not technically a millennial, I certainly needed a friend with a similar interest: food. I hoped that

---

162 Sherry Turkle, *Reclaiming Conversation*, 181.

maybe the app would match me with someone in the area, anyone in the area, who had the time and space to take me and all of my crap to a grocery store or burrito barn. I put a nice smiling picture of me up for the profile, along with this headline in hopes of attracting the local singles:

Hello there! My name is Niq.
I'm really hungry and I like pickup trucks!
Please come *pickup* me and my bike from the Denver International Airport.
Before midnight please and thanks!

Heck, this wasn't a date, but I would have been totally cool buying Taco Bell for whomever decided to show up! Jo and I had been together for a couple of years at this point, so I didn't think she'd mind me going out to get food with someone I didn't know, or at least I hoped she would be cool with it. After a few hours of vehemently swiping right, I still didn't have a match. Maybe my profile was too forward? So, I stopped swiping and called Jo and Tommy to tell them about my predicament. They just laughed and said I should use Uber Eats—but I was too cheap to be *that* hungry. The next half-dozen hours found me sleepily watching over my goods, finally getting them checked, and then boarding a plane that I hoped to God wouldn't be delayed.

A few weeks after arriving in Dayton, I was beginning to feel pretty settled into my new urban surroundings. I was sleeping in a bed, not on the floor of Denver's baggage claim with TSA babysitters watching my every move, and I was eating at least one meal each day to boot! It was actually quite nice.

Well, most of it was nice.

I suffer from a self-diagnosed condition called "agoraphobia," which essentially means that I begin to panic after residing in an urban area, without reprieve, for too long. So, after only a couple of days hanging around the church and my new apartment, I tried to get out of town. The problem was, there was so much town! It wasn't too long before I had explored most of the local bike paths and braved the crazy Ohioan drivers on some commuter roads, but they were all really flat and almost added to the anxiety created due to my agora phobia. I felt trapped.

You may be laughing at my stupidity, but step into my shoes here for a moment: 150 kilometers in a car might only take you an hour and thirty minutes to drive. Driving that far could easily take you out of most any sizable town, Dayton included, but 150 kilometers on a bike is a different story altogether. First of all, you've got to take plenty of fuel: food, water, and tire repair kits. It's not like that's really the biggest deal. I mean there are plenty of water fountains and super-markets around town which help ease the load, but then you have to do this thing called "pedal"—it's where you become the engine of the bike. I think that it might be harder than driving stick shift, not that stick shift is all that hard, but once you've ridden seventy-five kilome-ters, you really need to think about turning around to ride back home before the sun sets, or the rain hits, or those angry Ohioan drivers come out to getcha!

As you might be able to imagine, after several less-than-savory encounters with the locals while riding my bike, and with a moun-tain-shaped void in my heart, I got kind of bummed out being in "America's Heartland." On the contrary, my pal, Timmy, who had moved there at a similar time, really seemed to be enjoying himself. Every time we went to a get-together with lots of other people, he seemed to fit right in and genuinely have a good time. I, on the other hand, was stressed-out by the presence of just a few new people! Far too many of my evenings were spent alone in my apartment, reading, watching the Red Sox, and wishing I were somewhere else entirely. Nonetheless, I learned something from Timmy and several others who

I worked with that summer. Somehow, they had the ability to love in what I found to be uncomfortable situations. And that inspired me to perk-up and do the same even in an environment which I found so foreign and sometimes stressful.

When it came time to fly home four months later, I would be lying if I said I wasn't at least a little bit excited. I was going to see Jo and Ken again, two of my favorite people! One thing I forgot to mention is that my dear friend, Tyler, had taken an internship as well that summer, down in Chattanooga, Tennessee. But, instead of flying, he drove, taking a set of my dumbbells with him. I wanted to stay in shape there in the flatlands! We met up on my birthday at Kentucky's Red River Gorge to go rock climbing. Timmy came along, too, and so I got my weights from Tyler and brought them back with us to Dayton. Sadly, since none of us had a birthday for the rest of the summer, Tyler and I didn't meet up again. So, when it came time for me to return home, I wrapped my weights in shirts, socks, jackets, and towels, and put them both inside one of my carry-on backpacks.

A few days later, my friend, Paddy, the pastor I had been working with, dropped me off at the airport, and I waddled my way over to the counter to check-in my big yellow duffel bag and road bike. This time I didn't fly Front-Tear, so my big luggage was taken care of without problem. I walked over to the security line, showed the TSA agent my ticket and ID, and was waived right on through. *This is going great!* I thought, *There is hardly any line! I'm going to breeze right through all of this and be to the gate a couple hours early!* I set my backpacks down on the conveyor belt, took out my computer and phone, removed my shoes, and took off my belt (you know the drill). I walked through the metal detector and nothing beeped. Amazing, right? Soon, I would be sitting in the terminal writing another chapter for this book!

The moment I was through, however, the TSA fella watching the X-ray machine screen motioned to one of his coworkers, and subsequently his coworker motioned to me. "Sir," she said (which is a weird thing to be called at twenty-two), "sir, do you have any items you wish to declare?"

"No," I replied sheepishly.

"Sir, I'm going to have to ask you to come with me," she responded

So, barefoot and beltless, I walked around the corner, behind the conveyor belt and X-ray machine, holding my pants up so that they wouldn't fall. We went behind an office divider where she put on some latex gloves, picked up a long cotton Q-tip, and she swabbed on the inside of my cheek. She then put on a new pair of gloves and patted me down. At the same time, another TSA agent walked into our cubicle, struggling to carry one of my two backpacks from the conveyor belt. He set it down on the table, with a thud, and left. Then, my TSA agent asked if she could take a look inside the bag.

I don't know about you, but I didn't exactly know quite how to answer a question like that—it sounded more like a kindly-phrased demand to me—but was like, "Sure. Go for it." I knew I didn't have any firearms in there. No knives. No bombs. No camp stove fuel. No chainsaw. No water bottle filled with water. Nothing that TSA would think of as being bad. So my new friend opened up the drawstring on the top of my pack, lifted its cover, and held the bag as high as she could, upside down.

Underwear and T-shirts came falling down onto the table. A climbing shoe followed. My cycling jersey was next, escorted by a book or two. Then, "Thud!" out fell one nine-kilogram weight, closely followed by its twin.

On seeing this, Ms. TSA looked me in the eye and said sternly, "Sir, there are some things you just can't travel with. I mean, you know you can't take weights like this with you onto a plane, right?"

- ♡ -

Oh the truth she spoke—there are some things which we think are supposed to expedite our journeys and yet actually slow us down. There are things that we thought would make our lives easier and better, which actually made them all the more difficult. And there are some things we have to set aside to get to the other side. Put simply, sometimes we've got to skip the moving walkways and leave our weights behind.

You see, to be love more freely, we can't always be weighted down with who we once were. We can't always be weighted down with things which were perhaps good, yes, but that are no longer important to our forward momentum. We have to leave some things behind, good things no less, and not get caught up in our past if we want to progress into a more holistic future of only love.

I have a friend who always talks about when he ran a 100 kilometer race several years ago. Somehow everything in his life is connected to that singular event—every story revolves around that one day in his life. It's an impressive accomplishment to be sure; heck, I've never run more than twenty kilometers in a single session! But sometimes I wonder if he's so caught up reliving his past that he is neglecting to live in the present. He's traded in the new for his old. The thing is, God is always asking us to step into the new. Telling us that no matter what, we're redeemed, we're loved, and we have the opportunity, as Richard Rohr and Mike Morrell point out, "to accept that we're accepted and to go and live likewise."[163] We're accepted! We can leave our old selves behind and move into the new lives of love we were created to live.

Broken down, the whole idea of only love is that of movement. Progression from what we once were to who we are now becoming. Journeying from old to new. There is a certain freedom which comes

---

163 Richard Rohr & Mike Morrell, *The Divine Dance*, 109.

from knowing that you are loved, no matter what. Because if we're honest, new certainly doesn't mean perfect. We're all going to be infected with the virus of sin for as long as we humans are in charge.

I think that's a big part of why I like the idea of Jesus as a symbol that takes on the shortcomings of all humanity. God is who combats sin for us—because God *is* the law of love. As one of my undergraduate professors, Alden Thompson, put it, "love is the fulfilling of the law."[164] All of that stuff we read about in the Bible, with a bunch of messed up humans trying to do their own thing, was really God doing God's best to take them on a revelatory journey towards only love. Towards a love who is God fulfilling the law on behalf of all of humanity's shortcomings. Paul, in his spiritually-loaded gospel reminder to the Ephesians says as much:

> He chose us in him before the foundation of the cosmos, that we might be holy and immaculate before him in love, marking us out in advance for filial adoption to himself ... which he has caused to abound for us in all wisdom and understanding, making known to us the mystery of his will, which was his purpose in him, for a husbandry of the seasons' fullness, *to recapitulate all things in the Anointed, the things in the heavens and the things on earth.*[165]

You see, love left everything behind to become what it redeemed.
And we have the opportunity to do the same.

---

164 Alden Thompson, *Inspiration*, 116.

165 Ephesians 1:4-5, 8-10. Emphasis added.

22

LEARNING TO SKI AGAIN

I like new old things. I used to have a flatwater kayak that was old, but new to me.

I found it abandoned in the woods outside of my parent's home in South Dakota. For geographical context, they lived only ten or so kilometers from a big granite mountain sporting four really famous American faces. After discovering the boat, I left it there for several months, waiting for somebody to come and get it. It was grey. And since grey is a cool color, I figured it belonged to a pretty cool person.

When I came back to check on it the next time I was home, it was still there, still grey, and still cool. I drug it out of the woods and took it to the closest pond to see if it would float. Thankfully, it did.

By the time I went to college, a couple of years later, I had repainted it purple and enjoyed plenty of entertaining adventures in it, like lashing my legs to its hull so as to test out some whitewater rapids. Freshman year, I kept the boat in a friend's backyard because, well, it wouldn't fit in my dorm room. And so whenever I wanted to get it, I would call or text his parents ahead of time to get their "OK" before coming to pick it up.

One fateful spring night, Joel came up to my room and asked if he could borrow the kayak for the weekend. He worked in the videography department at school and was going to shoot a promo video for outdoor activities sponsored by the student association.

Now, Joel is a good friend of mine; he was in my wedding and stuff like that. So, I told him that if he really needed the boat, we'd need to get it that night because I was leaving right after class the next morning to go climb the beautiful Mount Rainier with some other friends. He said he really did need it, and so, at around 11:30 that fateful evening, we pulled up to my friend's parent's house. I didn't call or text ahead because I knew they both went to bed really early and didn't want to wake them—you know, to be considerate. So, instead, I just told Joel to be really quiet.

We snuck towards the backyard, tiptoeing all the way, proceeded through the gate—which didn't screech all that much when we opened it—and entered into the grassy backyard. Thankfully, they didn't have a dog or anything, so we were doing pretty well. Anyway, we grabbed the purple beauty from behind the shed and began to tiptoe our way back towards the road in front of the house where my faithful Gurdy was parked.

As we lifted the kayak onto the roof rack, we heard a noise from the front porch. I looked, and out into the porch light stepped my friend's dad, in his boxers, with a flashlight shining our direction.

Now, I neglected to mention this, but my pal's dad was also one of my professors. I had and still have a lot of respect for the guy. I even have a picture of him I won at a Christmas party sitting in my study. So, as you can imagine, when Joel and I saw him step onto the porch we started yelling his name: "PAUL!" we yelled in all-caps, "PAUL! IT'S NIQ AND JOEL! WE'RE JUST GETTING THE KAYAK!" He returned the yells by telling us Officer K and his entourage were on the way.

We rushed away in terror, looking down every adjoining street for cop cars—you could say we were pretty spooked.

The next morning I was up bright and early. Chad and Tyler were also up early. Because that's what you do when you are trying to earn a degree but also want to climb mountains.

As you know by now, these dudes are two of my best pals. In the fall, when we first met, we had explored some of our local rock climbing crags but got rained on a lot. Then in the winter, I proquired this free lift ticket to a local ski hill and went skiing for the first time (unless you count my road-ski with Tommy, which in that case would make it my second). Come springtime, we were getting pretty excited because we had a big goal in mind: We wanted to hike up Mount Rainier—a respectable 4392 meters tall. No easy way to the summit. The crown jewel of the western United States' Cascade volcanoes. The feather we all thought our caps needed.

And so, after our respective morning classes, we all piled into Tyler's little red, mid-90s Honda sedan with food, backpacks, and a deep thirst for some glacier-covered adventure.

After several hours of driving, we arrived at the park entrance.

Soon after, however, we realized that we had driven into a conundrum, a fiasco, a bad situation—whatever you want to call it. The road up to the trailhead had closed at least an hour before we arrived. We waited for close to another hour until someone, who was coming down off of the mountain, came to the gate, got out of his car, and walked over to the ranger station to get the key. After trading a roll of Ritz crackers with the guy in exchange for his letting us through, we finished our drive up to the trailhead, then quickly purchased our climbing permits from the self-serve kiosk before starting up the mountain just before midnight.

As you might have guessed, the sky was pitch black. Only the light of our headlamps and the occasional bit of moonlight peeking out behind the clouds aided us in our trek up a seemingly never-ending snowfield. It wasn't until around 3 a.m. that we sleepily stumbled across the alpine huts of Camp Muir and quietly showed ourselves into the first hut we saw. It was small but appeared to be completely vacant with three empty bunks, exactly the amount we needed.

We slept well that night. Really well, actually. Like, surprisingly well for as late as we had gone to bed. However, come 10 a.m., we woke up and quickly realized that we had neglected to set our alarms for around four, which is when we would have needed to get up if we wanted safe conditions traversing the mountain's glaciers. This, sadly, was only the first of many issues to surface that day.

I remember unzipping my sleeping bag and crawling out of my cocoon in what appeared to be a climbing-hut paradise. Colorful Buddhist prayer flags adorned the ceiling. Beautiful murals were painted on the surrounding walls. Extra glacier ropes, helmets, and ice axes, along with shelves filled with various books, dry food, and fuel canisters were only a fraction of what met our sleepy eyes. Unbeknownst to us, we had accidentally spent the night in the National Park Service's climbing ranger hut which, as it turns out, was kept full of emergency supplies for mountain rescues.

Thankfully, we didn't go to jail for breaking and entering, but we did get some curious looks from other climbers as we emerged from the hut into the blinding sunlight reflecting off of the snow all around us. It took a few minutes for us to gain our bearings, but eventually we could see enough to realize that the task ahead of us would take far more courage than the effort we had put in the night before. It was maybe around eleven that morning when we finally set off to tackle the second half of the mountain.

The upper 1300 meters of Rainier's east side is where glaciers begin to pose somewhat of an obstacle. It's also where our little hike began to get significantly more dangerous. The real danger of glacier travel is that there are these huge crevasses in the snow that you risk falling into. Some of the cracks are tens of meters deep and far too wide to jump across. If you get stuck inside, it can cost you your life. So, to avoid death, you have to tie your party all together with a rope and hope that if one of you falls in, the other two can use their ice axes and crampons to self-arrest in an attempt at keeping the entire group from getting permanently iced.

As we began crossing our first of several glaciers, we realized that the conditions were really bad, in part because we left an hour to noon. The sun was high and hot! Had we left at three or four that morning as planned, the snow wouldn't have been slushy and we wouldn't have had to turn around only 500 meters or so from the summit, just to make it back to camp before dark. Nevertheless, the conditions were really bad, we were really inexperienced, and, on top of that, I was realizing how bad of shape I was really in. It felt like we were trying to swim up a vertical pool! It was outlandish!

Now, the entire time we're walking up the mountain there were these really smart people who would whizz past us on their way down. Smart not only because they had left at 4 a.m., as we should have, but also because they had brought these things called "skis" along with them.

Alright, I know that some of you reading this book are sitting inside a sunny sunroom in a land where the temperature never drops below seventy. And because of your particular situation, maybe you have never heard of skis or skiing, let alone the white stuff many folks, myself included, know as "snow." If this is your context, let me be the first to tell you that this skiing business, despite the cold, is a whole lot of fun. Yet, as fun as it may be, I was relatively new to the sport at the time. Several months before this hike up Rainier, my good pal, Mason (who hates sleep but has a great heart), had gotten a brand new set of skis and conjoining ski boots for Christmas. Seeing that I didn't own a pair, and knowing that I had really only been sledding before, he gifted me his old skis and his old ski boots. Subsequently, I went to Goodwill and got somebody else's old ski poles and ski goggles to complement my friend's gift. I donned all the gear in my dorm room and looked at myself in the mirror. And let me tell you, I looked good! I was ready to conquer those slopes.

Unfortunately, the skis Mason had given me weren't just any kind of skis. They were these heavy, ugly, old park skis, meaning that they were intended for cool flips and hot tricks on a groomed track of fifteen years ago. Not thousands of meters of backcountry snowfields today. As I mentioned earlier, that winter I had gotten a free lift ticket for a local ski hill, and, since I had procured skis and everything else I needed to use them, I decided I would go. I went with some friends who told me I was doing really well for a first-time skier—but let's be honest, they were probably lying to make me feel all warm and fuzzy inside. So, at the very least, I was getting the hang of skiing, and got to feel all warm and fuzzy while doing it.

After that quite literal *crash course* on how to ski, I knew how to ski. Well, kind of. I could turn tight corners. I could jump off of rocks (I should say *flail* off rocks). But I felt pretty good for day one.

Fast forward three months to that attempt on Mount Rainier. We were sitting there at almost 4000 meters above sea-level, tired, mad, sad, but determined to come back soon with skis. I didn't care that I would have to lug an extra dozen kilograms up the mountain. I was going to come back. I was going to summit the darned thing. And I was going to ski back down to the car.

Five days later, we were back. Same crew. Same "can-do" spirit. But with new gear: I had packed the park skis.

Hiking up to the hut the next Saturday morning sucked, I'll admit. The extra pack weight was not fun, but we left the trailhead mid-morning instead of at 10 p.m., which really helped our spirits a lot. We didn't have to use headlamps, and it was even hot enough to take my shirt off! (A decision I later lived to regret because, well, sunburn.)

Also, by avoiding any fiasco getting into the park as we had the first time around, we saved an entire roll of Ritz crackers for our own consumption!

Although we moved at a slower pace due to our heavy burdens, we made it to the huts well before dinner time. My legs were sore, but my heart was soaring. After we settled into the actual climber's hut, which was nowhere near as fancy as the one set apart for the climbing rangers and their harrowing rescues, we went to bed. We slept nearly six hours before our alarms went off not a minute after midnight.

Our trip to the summit was fairly uneventful. No one fell into a crevasse. No slushy snow like the prior weekend's experience. No real problems whatsoever. We summited at around 8:30 that morning, not long after watching a gorgeous alpine sunrise from the east.

We took a few photos, then turned our gaze downwards to the parking lot nearly 3000 meters below. We hiked down past the most dangerous crevasse fields before strapping on our skis and snowboards. Thus, beginning what has remained the most memorable ski descent of my life.

Friends, this was no road flat enough to camp on. This was thousands upon thousands of meters of fresh vertical powder. Let that sink in. Close your eyes and picture the beautiful white slopes ... it was *paradise*.

As romantic as all of this sounds, and indeed it was, I want you to remember this very important detail: I had only skied once before. Well twice, I guess. Once as a toddler on the bunny hill, and the second time several months before our expedition while benefiting from that free lift ticket I had procured. While on both of those occasions I felt as though I had done a pretty good job at skiing, nothing can prepare one's thighs for thousands and thousands of meters of vertical descent on a massive ski hill that doesn't feel like it will ever end. Now, had this been my only problem, I think I could have managed just fine. But the length of the ski wasn't my only problem. I was also skiing with a backpack.

For those of you who may be obsessed with color, my backpack was bright neon green. It's the same one that TSA representative confiscated my dumbbells from. But I'll be honest, color and general travelability were the least of my concerns once I started skiing that afternoon. My backpack was filled with ice screws and a small rack, my climbing boots, an ice axe, a spare tent, my sleeping bag, several extra layers, a stove and fuel, avalanche gear complete with a foldable shovel, water, a seventy meter rope, food, sleeping mat, crampons, and, heck, maybe even a basketball. I don't remember! Now, if you don't know what some of those things are, don't worry. Just know that combined they are heavy! Dare I say, *very heavy*.

Frankly, the first thirty minutes or so of skiing took some adjustment, and my mistakes were plentiful. Several times I recall having to hike back up the hill, backpack and all, to collect a loose ski. I have some selfies I took during this stage in the descent, and I look pretty annoyed with myself probably because, well, I was pretty annoyed with myself! I lost my balance what seemed like countless times. It happened even during the easiest of sections! Every thirty seconds or so, I ended up with that beautiful white powder all up in my face! I could ski. I knew I could. On that ski hill only a few months prior I had made tight turns down steep tree runs and flailed off of big rocks! I knew how to ski! What was wrong with me?

The reason I fell, tripped, and rolled down Mount Rainier is because there is a big difference between skiing and skiing with a backpack. Fundamentally, they are the same thing. But practically, they can be very, very different.

That difference of experience between skiing with or without a backpack had me walking away from our Rainier trip reminded of the difference between the ten commandments that God is said to have given the ancient Hebrews and the new commandment Jesus talks about some time later. Practically, they are the same thing—meaning they can both have the same result.[166] But they look different, they certainly sound different, and, most importantly, *they feel different.* On the one hand, if you're an ancient Hebrew told to keep the ten, and you do, God says you'll live. But on the other, while it may seem simple to only love, it's really impossible. Putting everything above ourselves sounds easy—it's just one rule—but in practice it is actually much more difficult than the other, especially when we're so used to skiing without a backpack.

So, let me make this disclaimer right off the bat: Following the new commandment Jesus talks about is hard. Actually, following the new commandment Jesus talks about and demonstrates is *impossibly* hard, especially when we compare it to the commandments outlined in the Old Testament. Most days, if I try hard enough, I can probably keep all ten: I won't lie, I won't cheat on my partner, I'll be nice to my parents, I won't worship another god, and I'll work to make everyone equal on the seventh day (which then persuades me to do it the other six as well). I can actually do alright with that list. In fact, the more rules you throw at me, the easier it becomes for me to find a loophole. The more fine print you make available, the more likely I'll weasel my way through it to get the result I want. And love, the great ethical code, is but forgotten. Quite frankly, this is exactly what happened with the Hebrew religious leaders of Jesus' day. And now, dare I say, much of the modern church is repeating history.

---

166 See Skip MacCarthy, *In Granite or Ingrained?*, 146-147.

ut the new commandment Jesus provides requires perfection and can't do perfection. Maybe you can, and if so, I'd love to know more about how awesome you are. But I think I can speak for all of us when I say that we can't do perfection. When it comes to this new commandment, all I can do is work on progression and adjust my life to live more in-line with the new way of love that Jesus presents us with, eventually waking us to the realization that we ourselves are love because we're made in God's image.

In all reality, we've been talking about this new commandment since page one of *Only Love*. Check out what Jesus says in John's gospel: "A new commandment I give you: that you love one another. As I have loved you, so too must you love one another."[167] Mark conveys Jesus as saying something similar when confronted by a sneaky religious leader: "And you shall love the Lord your God out of your whole heart and out of your whole soul and out of your whole reason and out of your whole strength ... You shall love your neighbor as yourself. There is not another commandment greater than these."[168] Heck, even Matthew, as we saw a few chapters back, gets in on the action here: "You shall love the Lord your God with all your heart and with all your soul and with all your reason. This is the great and first commandment. The second is like it: You shall love your neighbor as yourself."[169]

As great as all of this sounds, just like skiing with a backpack takes adjustment, the new commandment of only love that we've talked about throughout this whole book takes some serious adjustment to get used to as well. It takes time to adjust our mindset from

---

167 John 13:34.

168 Mark 12:30-31.

169 Matthew 22:37-39.

commandments of "do's" and "don'ts" to "love" and "only love." It takes time for our minds to adjust to the realization that, because God is love, we are called to be Christ to those around us. It takes time to adjust to the realization that we are a part of this body of Christ. It takes time to transition our thinking from, *The only thing that matters is my relationship with God, vertically.* To, *The only thing that matters is that I be the love that God is to those I am confronted with every single day, horizontally.*[170]

It takes even more courage to admit that we won't ever really "get it." That even after we've skied Mount Rainier a thousand times, we'll still fall, we'll still lose a ski, we'll still get a face full of powder. Because being *only* love won't happen easily or all the time. It's a process, capstoned in humanity by the life Jesus lived.

The very idea of a God is but imagined and variable depending on who does the imagining; so I choose, like so many before me, to imagine God as love—for it requires us to see everything else in the same light. And it gives us the opportunity to partner with the divine, to become intertwined with the divine, in bringing the kingdom of heaven to earth. As Hans Urs Von Balthasar once wrote, "our own love … must take its direction from the model of the divine love."[171] The new covenant begins the divine work of peeling back the layers upon layers of sin in our lives and the lives of those around us, revealing how humanity was, is, and will always be.

Only love.

This new way of skiing tells us to start taking our cues from the love that is God. I mean, if we are cut from the cloth of Christ, are we not all glimmers of this same light? Are we not all sparks of such a

---

170 Andy Stanley points out in the fourteenth chapter of his book, *Irresistible*, 179-191.

171 Hans Urs Von Balthasar, *Dare We Hope "That All Men Be Saved"?*, 65.

divine love? I would argue that no matter who you are, no matter how wonderful you think you may be, no matter where you live, no matter the color of your skin, no matter how great you may think your country is, we're all as "pagan" as can be. We're no better than the next chap down the line and are all in need of divine refinement.[172]

Yet, God chooses *all* of us to share in the light of love. In all reality, that's what this whole book has been filled with: stories of people bringing sparks of the promised kingdom of divine love down into my life and the lives of those around me. Sometimes it's been friends and family. Sometimes strangers. Sometimes animals. Sometimes, even, myself. Because we're all a part of this divine dance with the creator of love. And whether we like it or not, even if we have to dig deep into our own stories to find it, we're all called to create such love, too—transforming feeling into *action*. Because love is not only what we were created to do but also who we are. We were all created to be love and we are all called to create it. We are called to be God to those around us by showing grace in an ungracious world.[173] We are called to only love.

The call is for you. The call is for me. The call is for all.

Because divine love *is* our love.

Let that sink in. God, Jesus, YHWH, Imanuel, the Divine, the Creator, the Infinite, the Truth, the Way, *Love* has called you to join in its mission to create more of itself. By living a life of love. With the sole mission of love. Fueled by the calling of love. For a kingdom of love. So that in the end, there will be *only love*.

This is our purpose—you and I were made to only love.

Let's go create this world *together*.

---

172 As suggested by Julie Ferwerda, *Raising Hell*, 66.

173 Philip Gulley & James Mulholland, *If Grace Is True*, 138.

23

NOW THAT WE'RE THROUGH

There is a particular exchange between Jesus and some of his closest friends which strikes me as profound. Jesus asks them, "[W]ho do you say I am?"[174] I love that question, but it hits me deep in my gut when I wonder what kind of answer I might get were I to direct it at Jesus.

"Jesus, who do you say I am?"

My generation has often said that we want to change our world, but activist marches and social media posts aren't concrete answers to the complex problems we face. And I'll be the first to admit that neither is writing a book. We all know life isn't perfect, but we don't mind looking good and simultaneously finding an easy way out of practically loving those around us. Volunteer hours are down across the United States because, well, maybe we don't want to get our hands dirty.[175] I'm guilty of fibbing volunteer hours for school assignments because "I didn't have time." And yet for some shameful reason, I am disgusted when someone wearing designer clothes posts a photo of

174 Matthew 16:15.

175 Marc Joseph, "America Does Not Have Enough Volunteers," *HuffPost*.

themselves picking up trash on a foreign beach. So, honestly, what kind of a hypocrite am I?

I know I'm not alone in realizing that there is a lack of practical love in my own life and in the world at large. Therefore our questions, if we wish to change, should be: How do we love? How do we create love? How do we create love within ourselves? How do we love our neighbors? How do we love the cosmic goodness from which we have sprung? How do we do the "doing" part of love?

If I can be so bold as to provide an answer: We love by giving a kid living out of his car a key to our new home. We love by keeping a finger puppet on our desks for the rest of the semester. We love by cheering on our suffering friends. We love by offering to pay for someone else's gas. We love by waiving a speeding ticket. We love by handing out clean washcloths. We love by fixing a broken clutch. *We love by being human.* Because humans were created to only love.

So, were I to ask Jesus, "Who do you say I am?" I can say with all confidence that he would reply, "You, Niq, are my creation, and you, Niq, are only love."

For infinite love sees only love.

This book was written to provide evidence for the kind of love life which we've all experienced glimpses of from time to time. A love that was outlined for us by Jesus when he asked us to only love. When he asked us to love first, second, and last. When he told us that we are love. When he gave us the opportunity to participate in his love *now*, when things aren't great, in anticipation of and for the creation of a better time to come. When he taught that we love God by loving those around us. People. Humans. Ourselves. Us. We.

NIQ RUUD

The complicated. Wonderful. Messy. Beautiful. Annoying. Inspiring. Nasty. Weird. Precious. Loved. People. Everywhere. All over the Earth.

For God so loved *all of the world*. That God gave *all of the love the divine had to offer*. So that in the end, there would be *only love*.

Friends, because of the incredible grace shown to all, we have no choice but to love even when loving seems impossible. We must love when loving *is* impossible. Because when we strive to love in the unconditional way God loves us, then our insignificant, tiny, boring, messy lives become a part of something so much bigger.

Elton Trueblood said, "The notion that we must choose between being service-centered and Christ-centered is a wholly confused notion. In fact, we shall not long continue to be service-centered if we cease to be Christ-centered."[176] You see, love is relational. It is a give-and-take. It's a feeling, yes, but it's also action. It is when we love and allow ourselves to be loved that we participate in the healing, the formation, and the renewal of Christ's body. A body so incomprehensibly large that Augustine questioned, "perhaps you have no need to be contained by anything, but rather contain everything yourself, because whatever you fill you contain, even as you fill it?"[177]

Looking back at my own life, as short and insignificant as it has been, I see that no matter the situation or circumstance love has always been there, bigger and better than anything I could ever have expected. That, as C.S. Lewis once mused, "good is everything and Heaven is everywhere."[178] You may say the analogies used throughout this book have been faulty, of course they have. I'm just as messed up as anyone. You may say this heretical idea of only love is simply youth-

---

176 Elton Trueblood, *The Incendiary Fellowship*, 116.

177 Augustine, *The Confessions*, 5-6.

178 C.S. Lewis, *The Great Divorce*, ix.

ful enthusiasm or fanciful devotion, and perhaps it is. I'm not the smartest bloke on the block. But to me, love is real. Perfect love has come to me through imperfect people. People just like you. People who chose, despite my shortcomings, to love without question. To love without expecting love in return. To *only love*, because that is what they were created to do.

And maybe I'm wrong. Maybe a God of only love doesn't exist. As much as I'd love to be, I'm not certain of it. How could I be? "Truth" is subjective and open to interpretation, and I'm no cosmic being of infinite knowledge. But I do have faith. And faith cannot exist in certainty. So, I choose to dream. I choose to hope. I choose to trust. I choose the uncertainty that my faith in love requires.

It is the creator of love who I choose to believe in. It *is* Love who I choose to believe in. And I can't wait to someday meet face to face.

Then again, *I suppose I already have.*

ACKNOWLEDGMENTS

Writing a book intertwining my theological framework with the experiences that have shaped such a worldview takes far more than just one person. I could write hundreds of pages detailing thanks for those who have not only pushed me spiritually, but also physically, mentally, and socially since my early years and throughout the writing process. Without these heroes, this book would never have made it to print. So, thank you *all*.

There have been many people, too, who I've never met or who have already passed, that have greatly impacted my worldview without their ever knowing it. They include Abraham Joshua Heschel, Brené Brown, Diana Butler Bass, Greg Boyd, Mahatma Gandhi, Martin Luther King Jr, Richard Rohr, the apostle Paul, and especially Jesus. Thank you all for teaching me from afar what God looks like up close.

I also want to thank Rafael Polendo and the good folks out at Quoir for taking a chance on me as a first-time author. Your grace throughout has made the publishing process gratifying, to say the least. Thanks also to my editor, Anna Rhea. Your keen eye and listening ear helped shape my final drafts into something worth reading. I am also indebted to the handful of friends and family members who muddled through some truly horrendous early versions of this manuscript and provided their invaluable perspectives. This book is all the better because of you.

Lastly, I want to share several particular tokens of gratitude to some very special people who have had a greater influence on me, and subsequently this book, than they may ever know. First, to Jo, for putting up with all of the late nights when I didn't come to bed until early in the morning while working on this book—know that you are the reason I rise each day. Kate, for embracing the only love ideal when we were just teenagers. Paddy, for telling me not to give up even when someone thinks I may be too radical. Chad, for sharing your whole heart with me. Tyler, for stretching me. Mason, for your adventurous soul. Al, for your confidence. Joel, for your vulnerability. Tommy, for always being there to bounce ideas off of. Professors Alden Thompson, Darold Bigger, Dave Thomas, Mathilde Frey, Paul Dybdahl, and Pedrito Maynard-Reid for your theological molding during undergrad. Mom and Dad, for *everything*.

You have all taught me where to find God—thank you for being only love to me.

— **Niq Ruud**

BIBLIOGRAPHY OF WORKS CITED

Augustine. *The Confessions.* Translated by David V. Meconi, SJ. San Francisco, CA: Ignatius, 2012.

———. *The Retractions.* Translated by M. Inez Bogan, RSM. Baltimore, MD: Catholic University of America Press, 2010.

Baldwin, James. "Letter from a Region in My Mind." *The New Yorker* (17 November 1962). https://www.newyorker.com/magazine/1962/11/17/letter-from-a-region-in-my-mind.

Bass, Diana Butler. *Grounded: Finding God in the World—A Spiritual Revolution.* New York, NY: HarperOne, 2015.

Bell, Rob. *Love Wins: A Book About Heaven, Hell, and the Fate of Every Person Who Ever Lived.* New York, NY: HarperOne, 2011.

Bigger, Darold. *A Time to Forgive: One Family's Journey After the Murder of Their Daughter.* Nampa, ID: Pacific Press, 2015.

Boring, M. Eugene. "The Language of Universal Salvation in Paul." *Journal of Biblical Literature* 105, no. 2 (1986): 269-292.

Boyd, Gregory A. *Cross Vision: How the Crucifixion of Jesus Makes Sense of Old Testament Violence.* Minneapolis, MN: Fortress, 2017.

———. *Inspired Imperfection: How the Bible's Problems Enhance its Divine Authority.* Minneapolis, MN: Fortress, 2020.

———. *The Crucifixion of the Warrior God: Interpreting the Old Testament's Violent Portraits of God in Light of the Cross.* Minneapolis, MN: Fortress, 2017.

Brown, Brené. *Daring Greatly: How the Courage to Be Vulnerable Transforms the Way We Live, Love, Parent, and Lead.* New York, NY: Avery, 2012.

———. *Rising Strong: How the Ability to Reset Transforms the Way We Live, Love, Parent, and Lead.* New York, NY: Random House, 2017.

Chan, Francis, and Preston Sprinkle. *Erasing Hell: What God said about Eternity, and the Things we've Made Up.* Colorado Springs, CO: David C Cook, 2011.

Dawkins, Richard. *The God Delusion.* Boston, MA: First Mariner, 2008.

Du Mez, Kristin Kobes. *Jesus and John Wayne: How White Evangelicals Corrupted a Faith and Fractured a Nation.* New York, NY: Liveright, 2020.

Eng, Ronald, editor. *Mountaineering: The Freedom of the Hills.* Eighth Edition. Seattle, WA: The Mountaineers, 2015.

Ferwerda, Julie. *Raising Hell: Christianity's Most Controversial Doctrine put under Fire.* Lander, WY: Vagabond, 2011.

Giglio, Louie. *Goliath Must Fall: Winning the Battle Against Your Giants.* Nashville, TN: W Publishing, 2017.

Goff, Bob. *Everybody, Always: Becoming Love in a World Full of Setbacks and Difficult People.* Nashville, TN: Nelson Books, 2018.

———. *Live in Grace, Walk in Love: A 365-Day Journey.* Nashville, TN: Nelson Books, 2019.

Grenz, Stanley J. *Renewing the Center: Evangelical Theology in a Post-Theological Era.* Grand Rapids, MI: Baker, 2000.

Gudme, Anne Katrine de Hemmer. "Perspectives on the Care and Feeding of the Gods in the Hebrew Bible." *Scandinavian Journal of the Old Testament* 28, no. 2 (2014): 170-182.

Gulley, Philip, and James Mulholland. *If Grace Is True: Why God Will Save Every Person.* New York, NY: HarperOne, 2003.

Hansen, David. *The Art of Pastoring: Ministry Without All the Answers.* Revised Edition. Downers Grove, IL: InterVarsity, 2012.

Hart, David Bentley. *That All Shall Be Saved: Heaven, Hell & Universal Salvation.* New Haven, CT: Yale University Press, 2019.

Heschel, Abraham Joshua. *The Prophets.* New York, NY: Perennial, 2001.

———. *The Sabbath: Its Meaning for Modern Man.* Boston, MA: Shambhala, 2003.

Hick, John. "A Pluralist View." In *Four Views on Salvation in a Pluralistic World,* edited by Stanley Gundry, Dennis Okholm, and Timothy Phillips, 29-59. Grand Rapids, MI: Zondervan, 1996.

Joseph, Marc. "America Does Not Have Enough Volunteers." *HuffPost* (31 January 2017). www.huffpost.com/entry/america-does-not-have-eno_b_9032152.

Jersak, Bradley. *Her Gates Will Never Be Shut: Hope, Hell, and the New Jerusalem.* Eugene, OR: Wipf & Stock, 2009.

Keener, Craig. *The IVP Bible Background Commentary: New Testament.* Second Edition. Downers Grove, IL: InterVarsity, 2014.

King, Martin Luther. *Strength to Love.* Boston, MA. Beacon, 2019.

Korpman, Matthew J. *Saying No to God: A Radical Approach to Reading the Bible Faithfully.* Orange, CA: Quoir, 2019.

Langberg, Diane. *Suffering and the Heart of God: How Trauma Destroys and Christ Restores.* Greensboro, NC: New Growth, 2015.

Lewis, C.S. *Mere Christianity.* New York, NY: HarperCollins, 2001.

———. *The Great Divorce.* New York, NY: HarperCollins, 2001.

MacCarthy, Skip. *In Granite or Ingrained? What the old and new Covenants reveal about the Gospel, the Law, and the Sabbath.* Berrien Springs, MI: Andrews University Press, 2007.

Mackie, Tim, and Jon Collins. "Character of God: Exodus 34:6-7." *BibleProject* (30 June 2020): www.youtube.com/watch?v=nxwzq1PJImM.

McCaulley, Esau. *Reading While Black: African American Biblical Interpretation as an Exercise in Hope.* Downers Grove, IL: InterVarsity, 2020.

Muddiman, John, and John Barton, editors. *The Oxford Bible Commentary: The Pauline Epistles.* New York, NY: Oxford University Press, 2001.

Origen. *On First Principles.* Translated by G.W. Butterworth. Notre Dame, IN: Ave Maria, 2013.

Parry, Robin A, and Ilaria L.E Ramelli. *A Larger Hope? Volume 2: Universal Salvation from the Reformation to the Nineteenth Century.* Eugene, OR: Cascade, 2019.

———. "A Universalist View." In *Four Views on Hell*, Second Edition edited by Stanley Gundry and Preston Sprinkle, 101-127. Grand Rapids, MI: Zondervan, 2016.

Ramelli, Ilaria L.E. *A Larger Hope? Volume 1: Universal Salvation from Christian Beginnings to Julian of Norwich.* Eugene, OR: Cascade, 2019.

Richards, E, and Richard James. *Misreading Scripture with Individualistic Eyes: Patronage, Honor, and Shame in the Biblical World.* Downers Grove, IL: InterVarsity, 2020.

Pinnock, Clark H. "An Inclusivist View." In *Four Views on Salvation in a Pluralistic World,* edited by Stanley Gundry, Dennis Okholm, and Timothy Phillips, 95-125. Grand Rapids, MI: Zondervan, 1996.

Robinson, John A.T. *In the End, God ... : A Study of the Christian Doctrine of the Last Things.* Special Edition edited by Robin Parry. Eugene, OR: Cascade, 2011.

Rohr, Richard, and Mike Morrell. *The Divine Dance: The Trinity and Your Transformation.* New Kensington, PA: Whitaker, 2016.

———. *The Universal Christ: How a Forgotten Reality can Change Everything we See, Hope for and Believe.* London, UK: SPCK, 2019.

Ruud, Niq. "Everything Over God." *Spectrum Magazine* (6 July 2020). www.spectrummagazine.org/views/2020/everything-over-god.

———, and Jordan Tamaleaa. "Strangers as Saviors." *The Young Project Podcast* (15 October 2019). www.podcasts.apple.com/us/podcast/e1-strangers-as-saviors/id1482587614?i=1000453574237.

Sire, James W. *The Universe Next Door: A Basic Worldview Catalog.* Fifth Edition. Downers Grove, IL: InterVarsity, 2009.

Smith, Huston. *The Soul of Christianity: Restoring the Great Tradition.* San Francisco, CA: HarperCollins, 2005.

Stanley, Andy. *Irresistible: Reclaiming the New that Jesus Unleashed for the World.* Grand Rapids, MI: Zondervan, 2020.

Stendahl, Krister. "The Apostle Paul and the Introspective Conscience of the West." *Harvard Theological Review* 56, no. 3 (1963): 199-215.

Talbott, Thomas. *The Inescapable Love of God.* Second Edition. Eugene, OR: Cascade, 2014.

Teilhard de Chardin, Pierre. *The Divine Milieu.* New York, NY: Harper & Row, 1965.

Thompson, Alden. *Inspiration: Hard Questions, Honest Answers.* Hagerstown, MD: Review and Herald, 1991.

————. *Who's Afraid of the Old Testament God?* Fifth Edition. Gonzalez, FL: Energion, 2011.

Trueblood, Elton. *The Incendiary Fellowship.* New York, NY: Harper & Row, 1967.

Turkle, Sherry. *Reclaiming Conversation: The Power of Talk in a Digital Age.* New York, NY: Penguin, 2016.

Von Balthasar, Hans. *Dare We Hope "That All Men Be Saved"?* Second Edition translated by David Kipp and Lothar Krauth. San Francisco, CA: Ignatius, 2014.

Walton, John H. *Ancient Near Eastern Thought and the Old Testament: Introducing the Conceptual World of the Hebrew Bible.* Grand Rapids, MI: Baker, 2018.

————, Victor H. Matthews, and Mark W. Chavalas. *The IVP Bible Background Commentary: Old Testament.* Downers Grove, IL: InterVarsity, 2000.

White, Ellen G. *Testimonies for the Church*, Volume Five. Mountain View, CA: Pacific Press, 1948.

Wolterstorff, Nicholas. *Lament for a Son.* Grand Rapids, MI: Eerdmans, 1987.

Wright, N.T. *How God Became King: The Forgotten Story of the Gospels.* New York, NY: HarperOne, 2012.

————. "Mind, Spirit, Soul and Body: All for One and One for All Reflections on Paul's Anthropology in his Complex Contexts." *NTWrightPage* (18 March 2011). www.ntwrightpage.com/2016/07/12/mind-spirit-soul-and-body.

————. *Surprised by Hope: Rethinking Heaven, the Resurrection, and the Mission of the Church.* New York, NY: HarperOne, 2008.

————, and Michael F. Bird. *The New Testament in Its World: An Introduction to the History, Literature, and Theology of the First Christians.* Grand Rapids, MI: Zondervan, 2019.

Yancey, Philip. *What's So Amazing About Grace?* Grand Rapids, MI: Zondervan, 1997.

For more information about Niq Ruud,
or to contact him for speaking engagements,
please visit *www.NiqRuud.com*

 QUOIR

Many voices. One message.

Quoir is a boutique publisher
with a singular message: *Christ is all.*
Venture beyond your boundaries to discover Christ
in ways you never thought possible.

For more information, please visit
www.quoir.com

GPSIA information can be obtained
at www.ICGtesting.com
Printed in the USA
LVHW051306241121
704206LV00003B/6

9 781938 480980